by
Ed Fischer

Adventure Publications, Inc.
Cambridge, Minnesota

Dedicated to Northstars Joe and Sally, wild and wonderful.

Text and illustrations copyright 2006 by Ed Fischer

Cover and book design by Jonathan Norberg

10 9 8 7 6 5 4 3

Published by Adventure Publications, Inc.
820 Cleveland Street South
Cambridge, MN 55008
1-800-678-7006
www.adventurepublications.net

ISBN: 978-1-59193-142-3

Ah! Camping! Hiking! Canoeing! Fishing! Hunting! Bugs! Cold! Rain! Aching muscles! Dirt! Stink! The GREAT outdoors. What makes it great? Cool, clean, crisp air. Seeing God's work all around you. Meaningful time with family and friends. Great nights. Great mornings. Great views. Songs around the campfire and hearty laughter. Laughter just naturally goes with the adventure and the reason for this book. Laugh at those things that go with the territory. Because outdoors people are special and industrious! Just ask anyone who couldn't get out of their tent because the zipper was stuck. Or the guy who had a raccoon take his car keys. Read. Laugh. Look at the photos from the trip one more time.

Bonus: Check out the flip art in the corner!

The loaded minivan pulled into the only remaining campsite. Four children leaped from the vehicle and began feverishly unloading gear and setting up the tent. They rushed to gather firewood, while the parents set up the camp stove and cooking utensils.

A nearby camper marveled to the youngsters' father, "That, sir, is some display of teamwork."

The father replied, "I have a system—no one goes to the bathroom until the camp is set up."

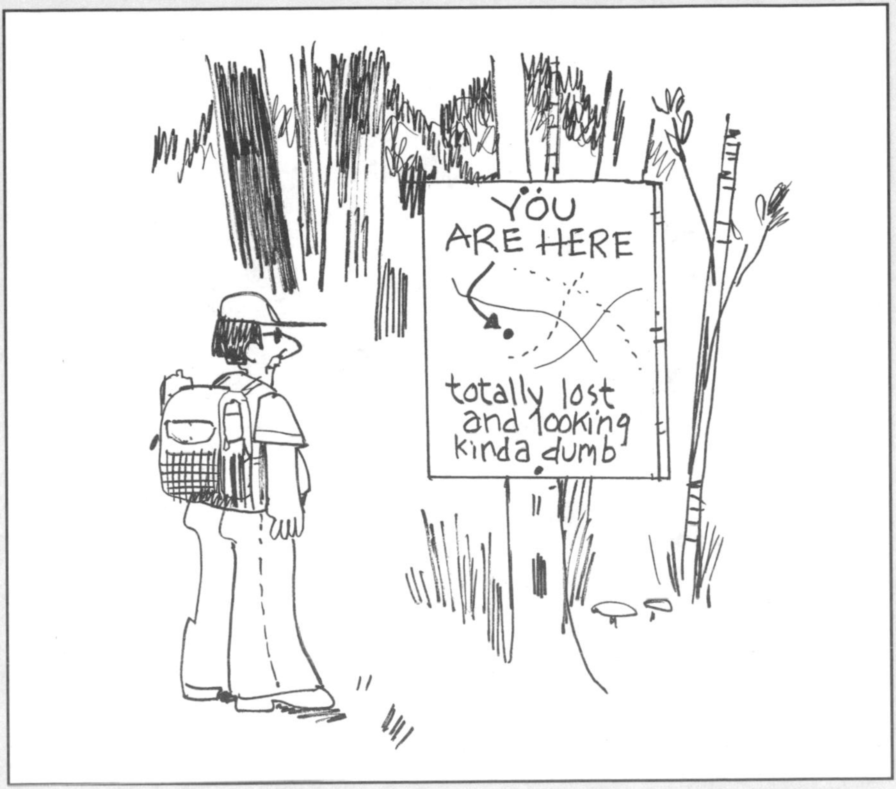
YOU ARE HERE
totally lost and looking kinda dumb

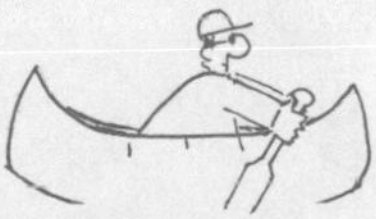

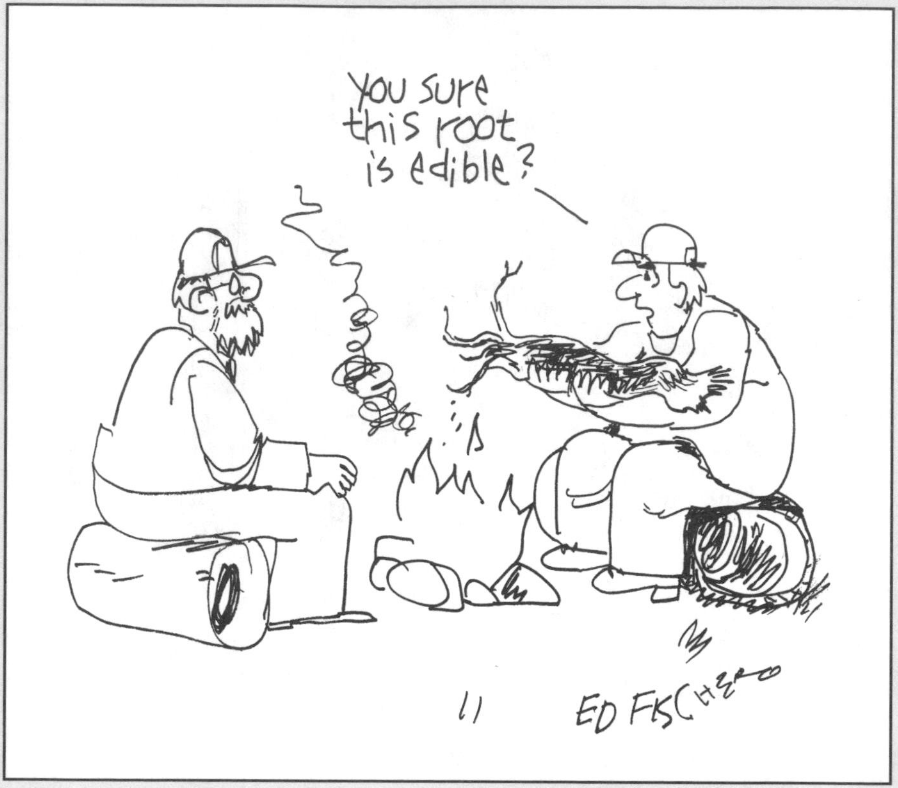
you sure
this root
is edible?
ED FISCHER

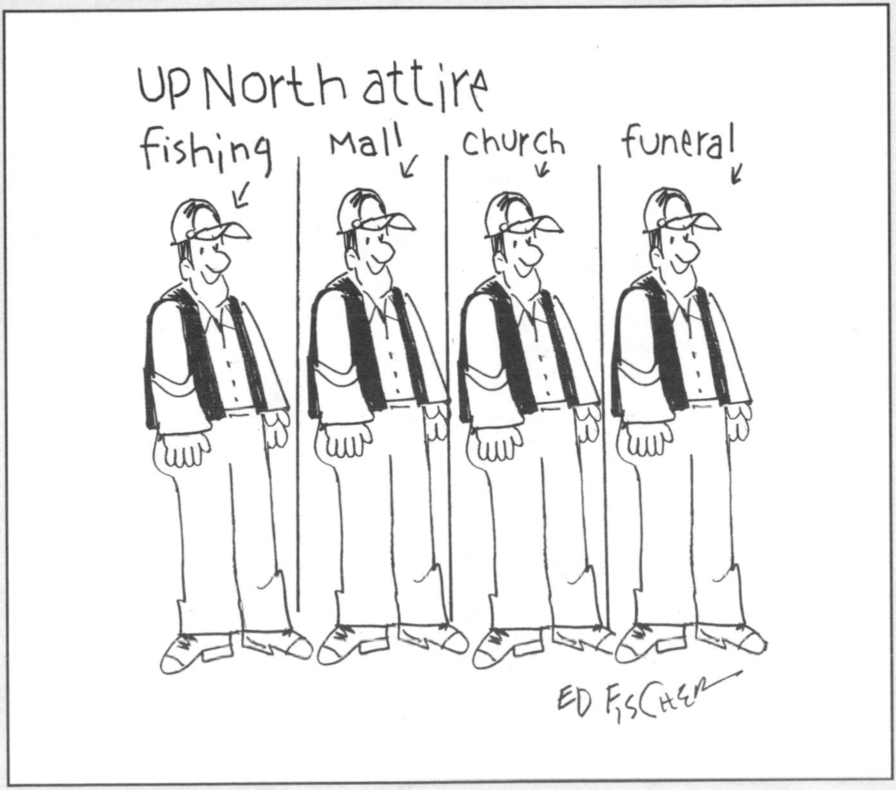
UP North attire
fishing
Mall
church
funeral
ED FISCHER

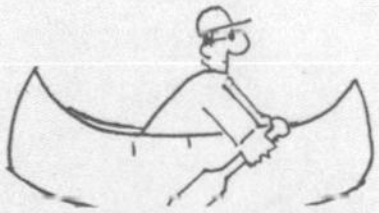

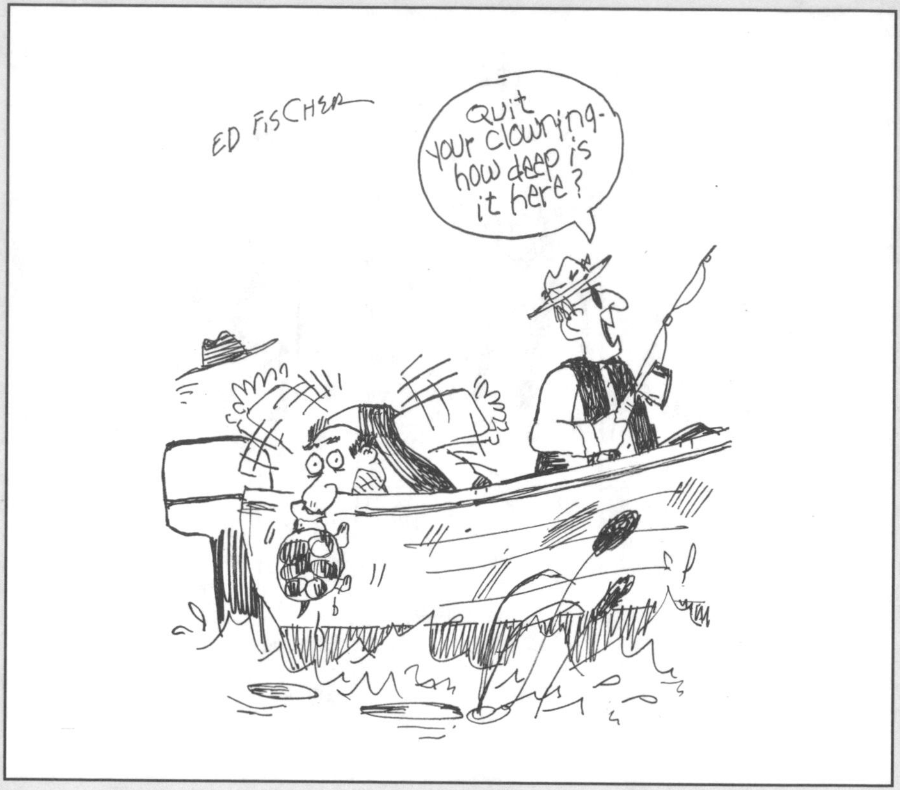
ED FISCHER
Quit your clowning- how deep is it here?

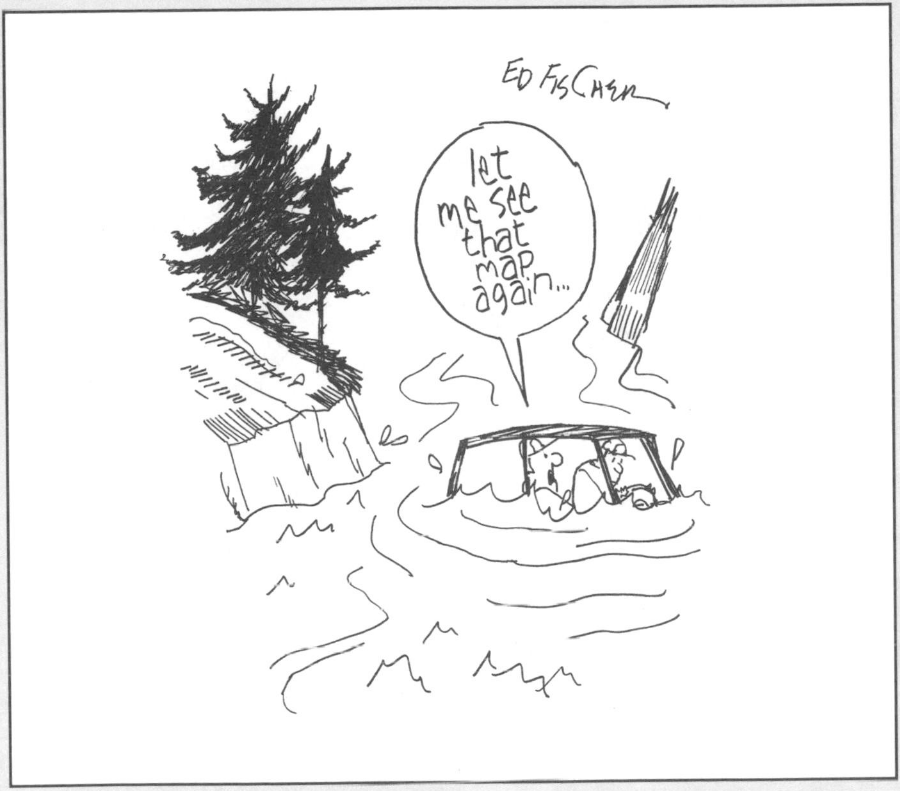
ED FISCHER
let me see that map again...

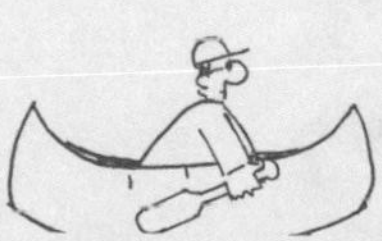

Dipnet Doug and a friend went fishing in Canada. They caught one fish between the two of them. When they got back Doug said, "Crapola! Adding up everything right here, that fish cost us a thousand dollars."

"Jeez Louise," said the friend. "Good thing we didn't catch any more fish."

Olaf and Oscar tried using the cookbook in the cabin to make some new kind of hotdishes. They had to give up. Every single recipe started with "Take a clean dish."

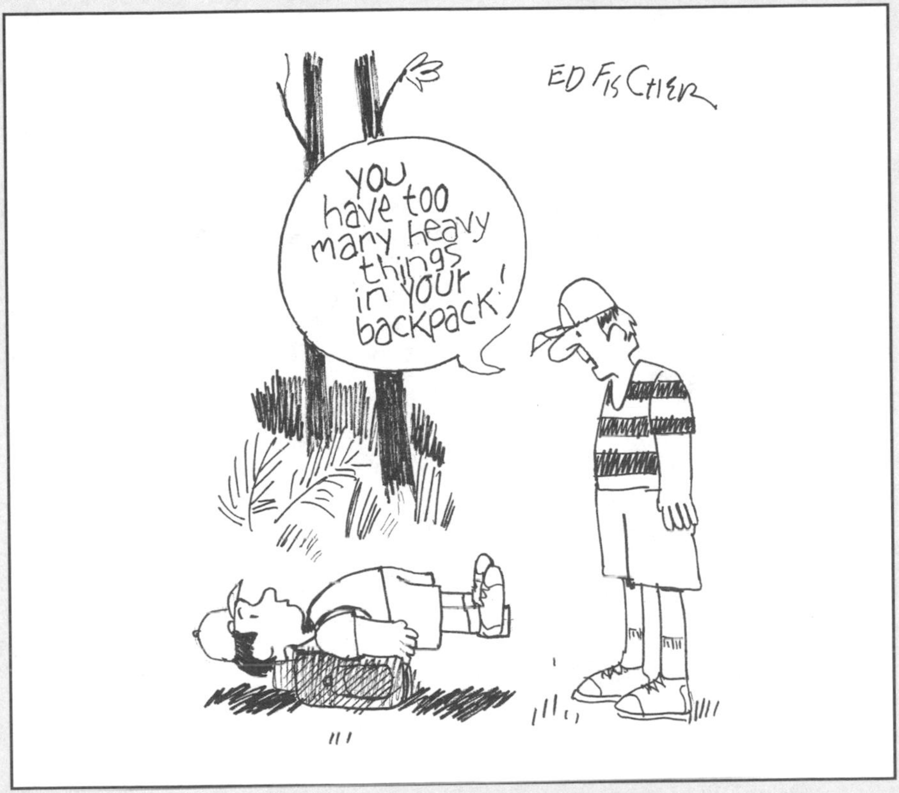
ED FISCHER
YOU have too many heavy things in YOUR backpack!

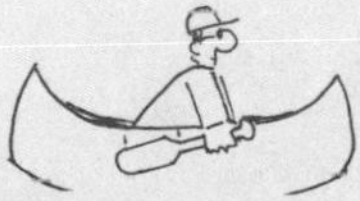

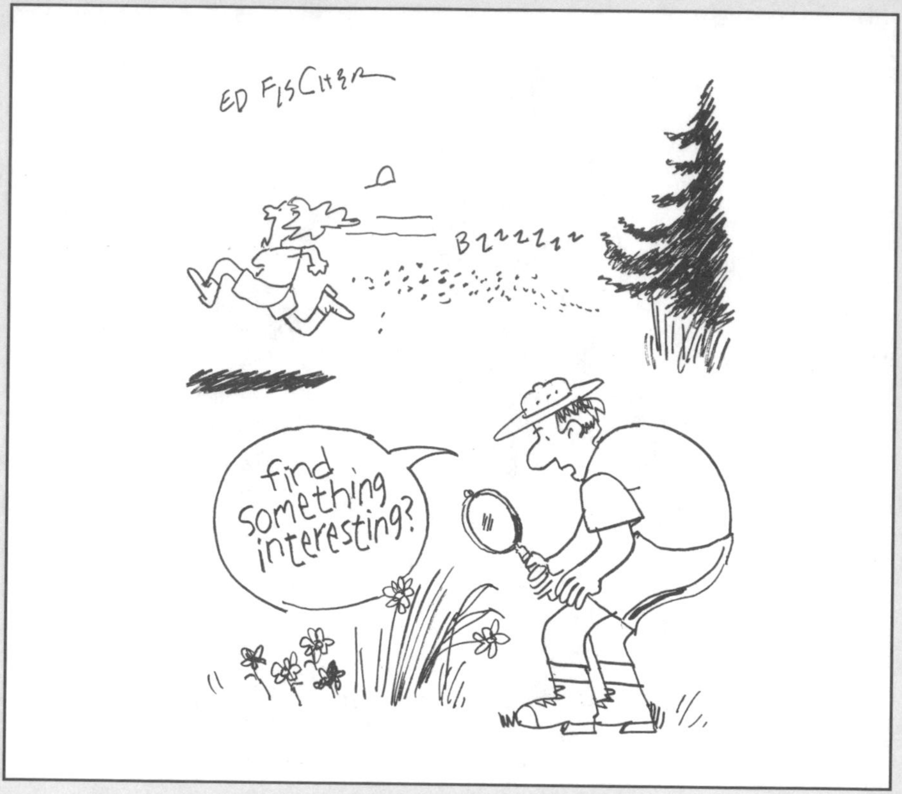
ED FISCHER
BZZZZZZZ
find something interesting?

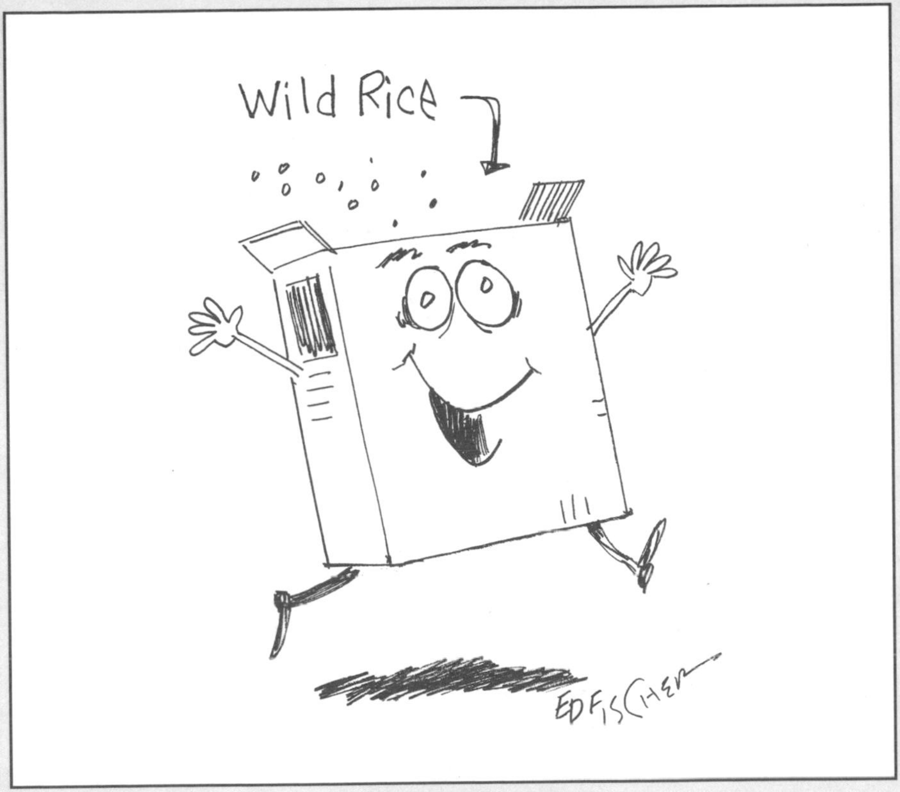
Wild Rice
ED FISCHER

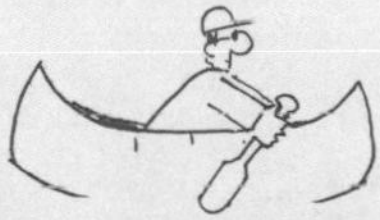

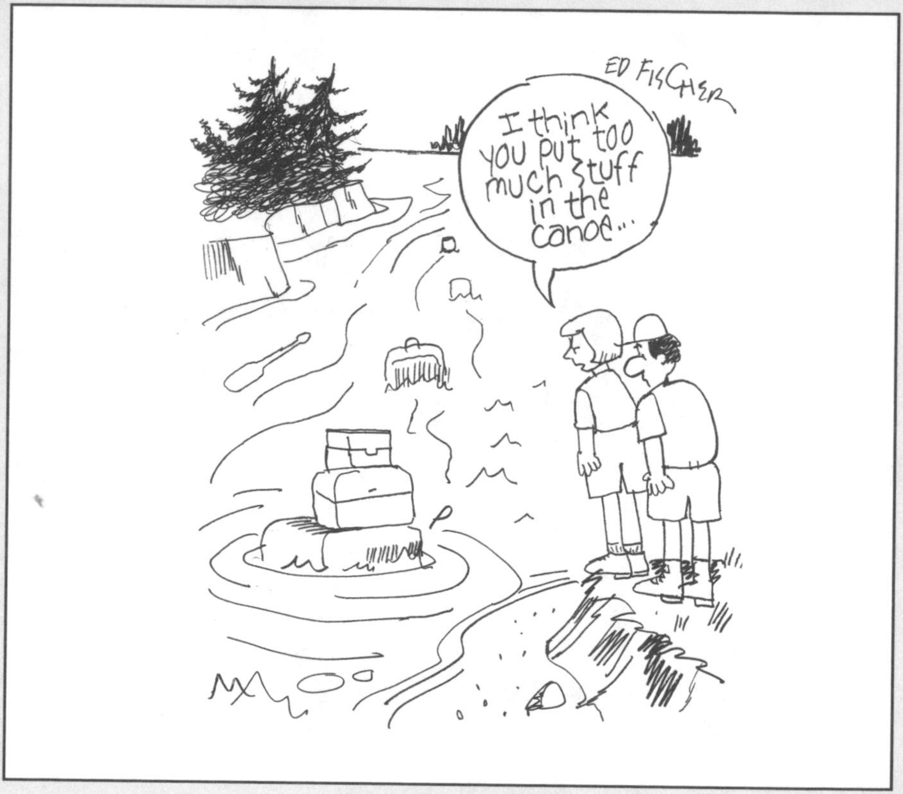
ED FISCHER
I think you put too much stuff in the canoe...

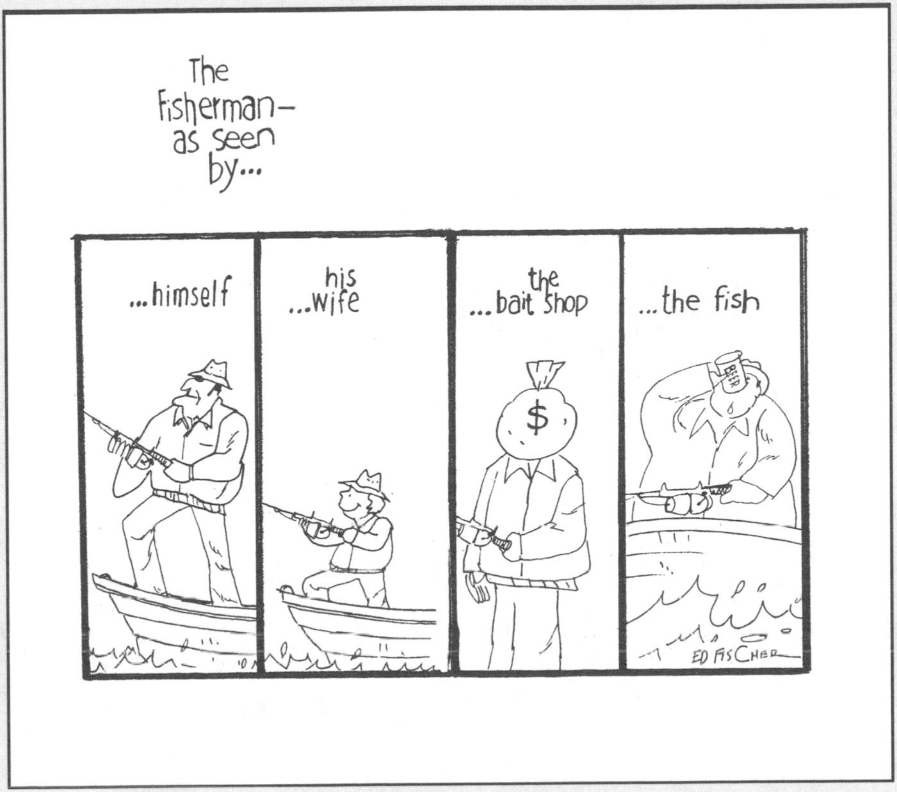
The Fisherman– as seen by...
...himself
his ...wife
the ...bait shop
$
...the fish
BEER
ED FISCHER

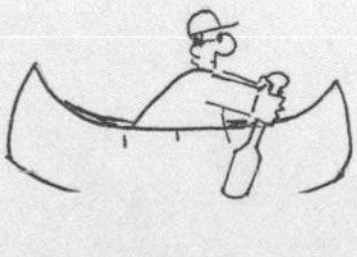

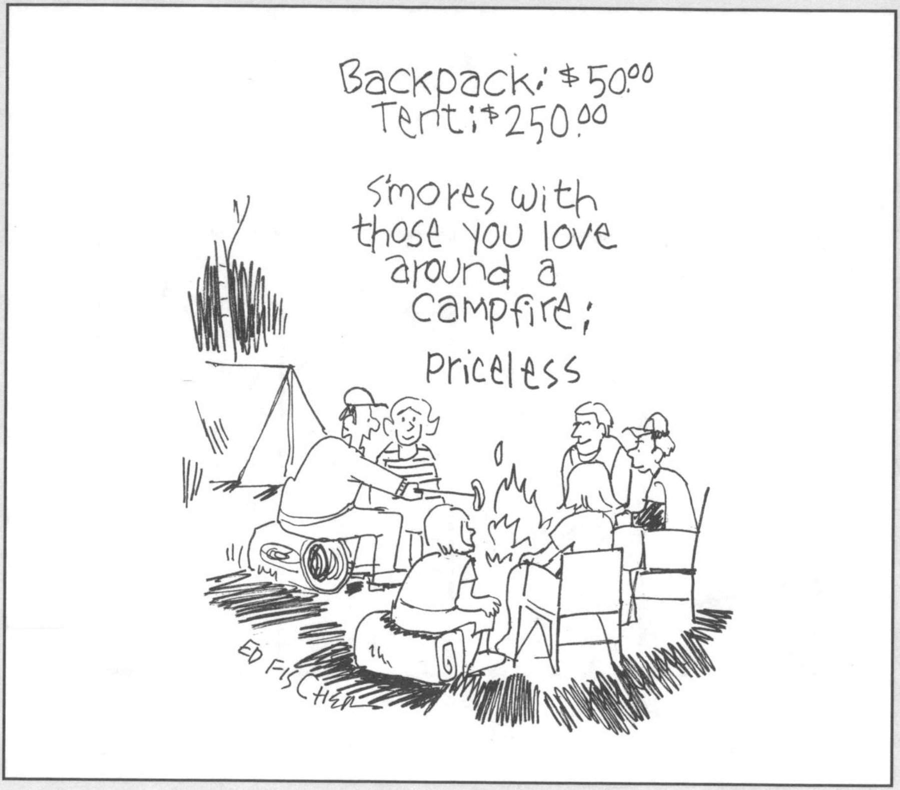
Backpack: $50.00
Tent: $250.00
S'mores with those you love around a campfire: priceless
ED FISCHER

Skeeter's neighbor says when her kids come back from camping, they don't leave a ring around the tub. They leave a ring around the room.

Lars loves to hunt, but he doesn't own a gun. He drives to a deer crossing sign and waits in his truck.

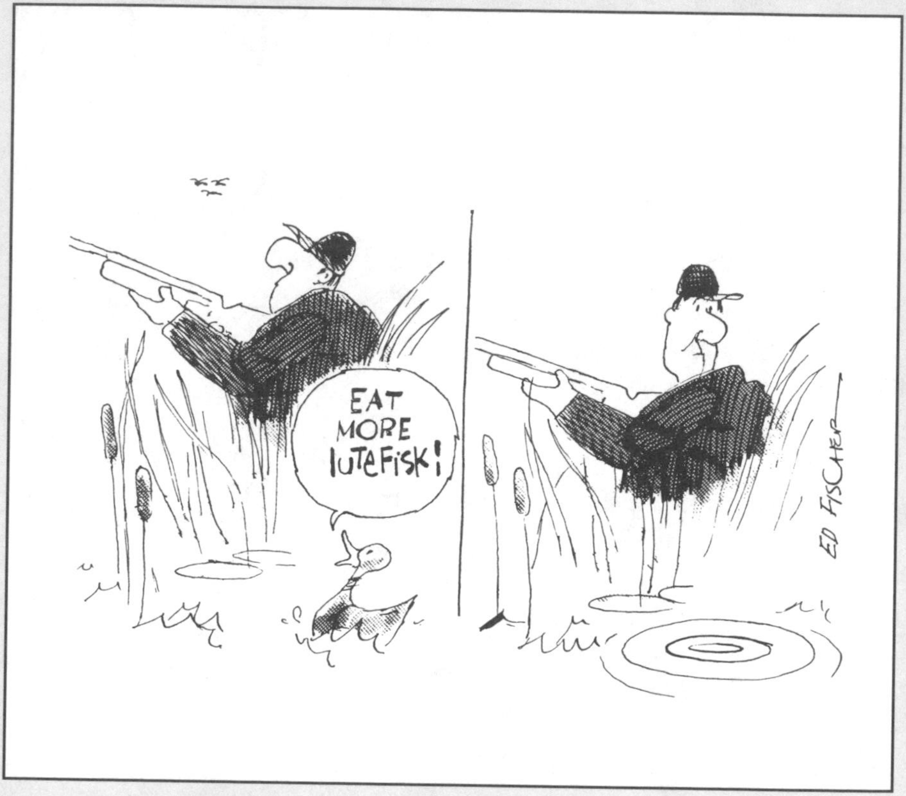
EAT MORE luteFisk!
ED FISCHER

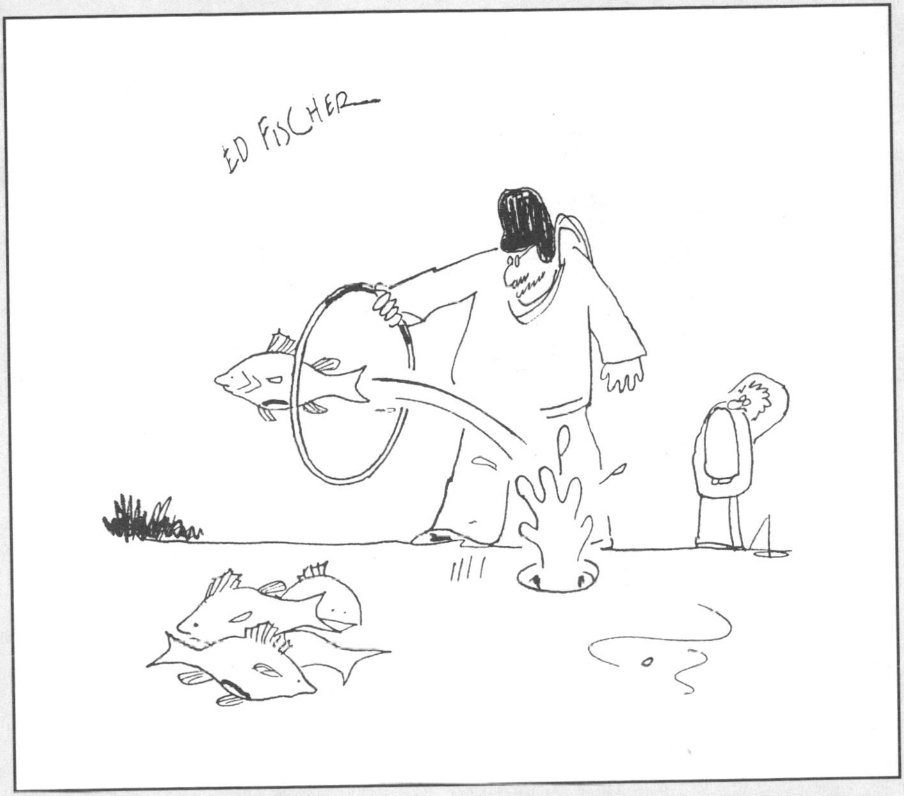
ED FISCHER

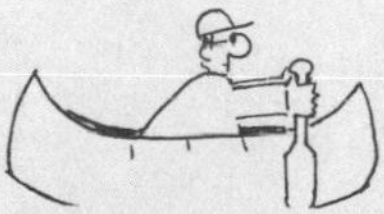

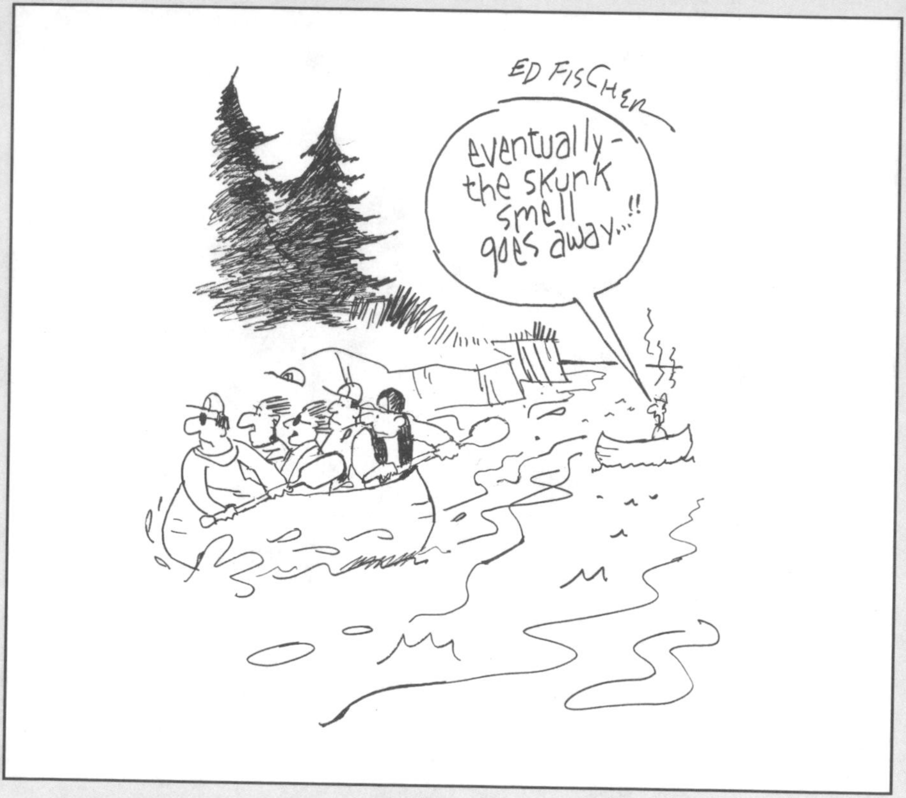
ED FISCHER
eventually - the skunk smell goes away...!!

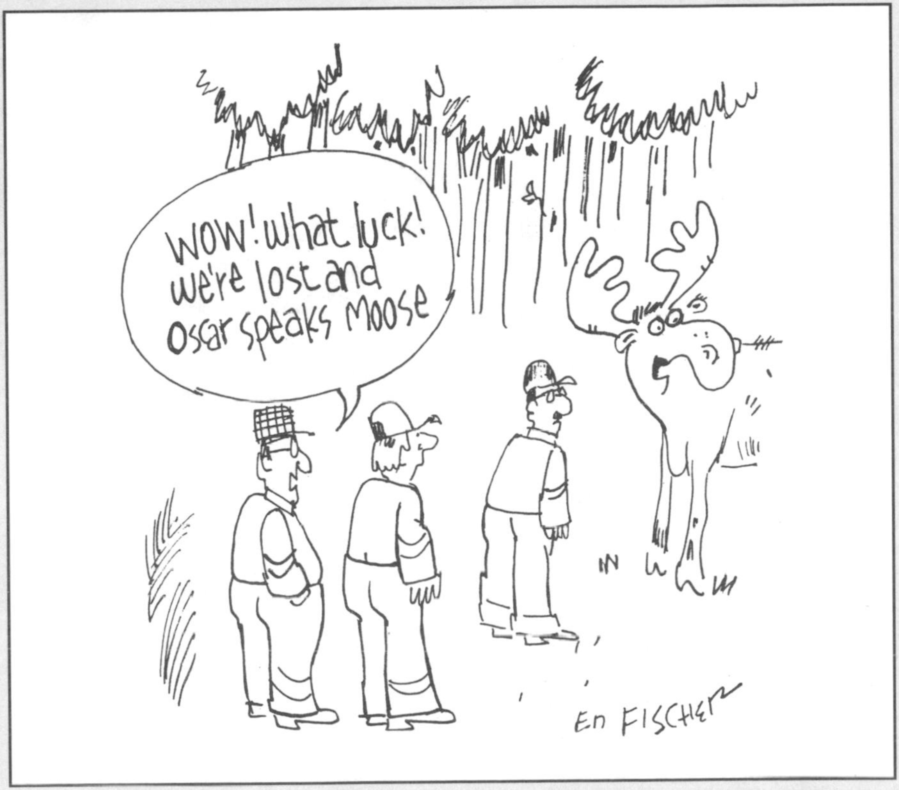
WOW! what luck! we're lost and Oscar speaks Moose
ED FISCHER

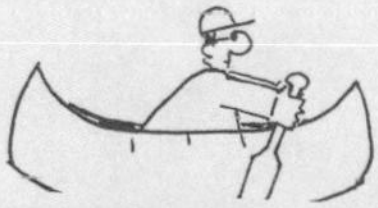

A hiker in the northwoods encounters a grasshopper on the trail. Feeling playful, he bends over the little green creature and says, "Hey, little guy, do you know they named an alcoholic drink after you?"

"No kidding," says the grasshopper. "They have a drink named Ed?"

Rusty bragged he could swim across Burnt Finger Lake. He couldn't make it. He swam halfway across and had to come back.

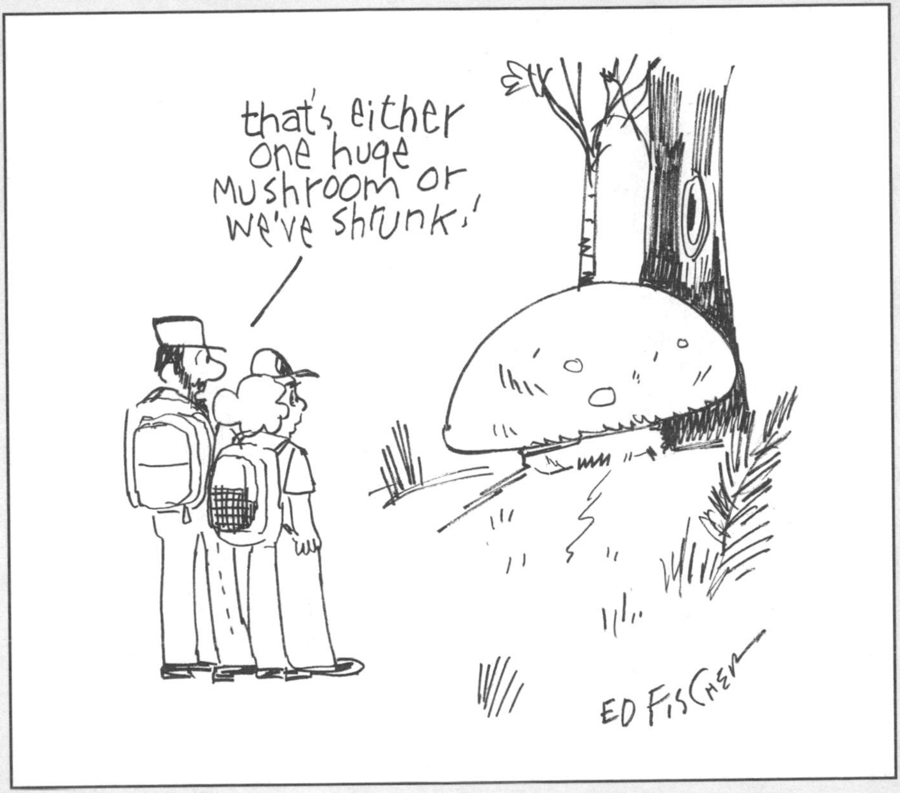
that's either one huge mushroom or we've shrunk!
ED FISCHER

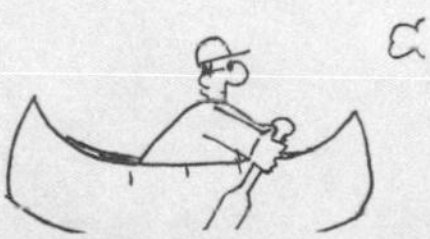

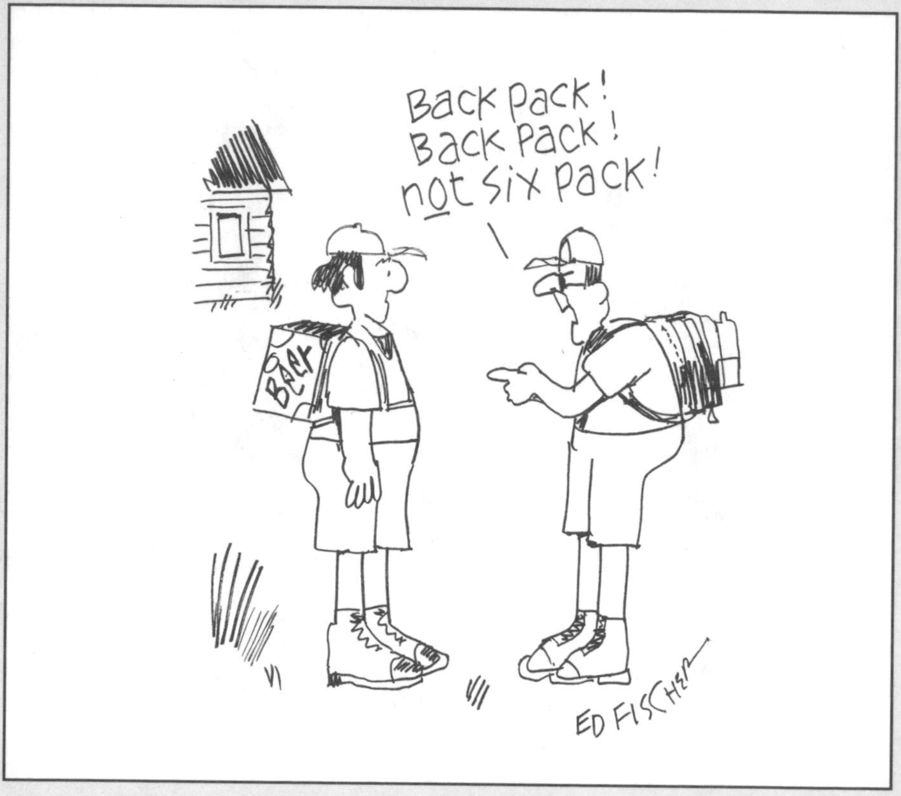

Back Pack!
Back Pack!
not six Pack!
Beer
ED FISCHER

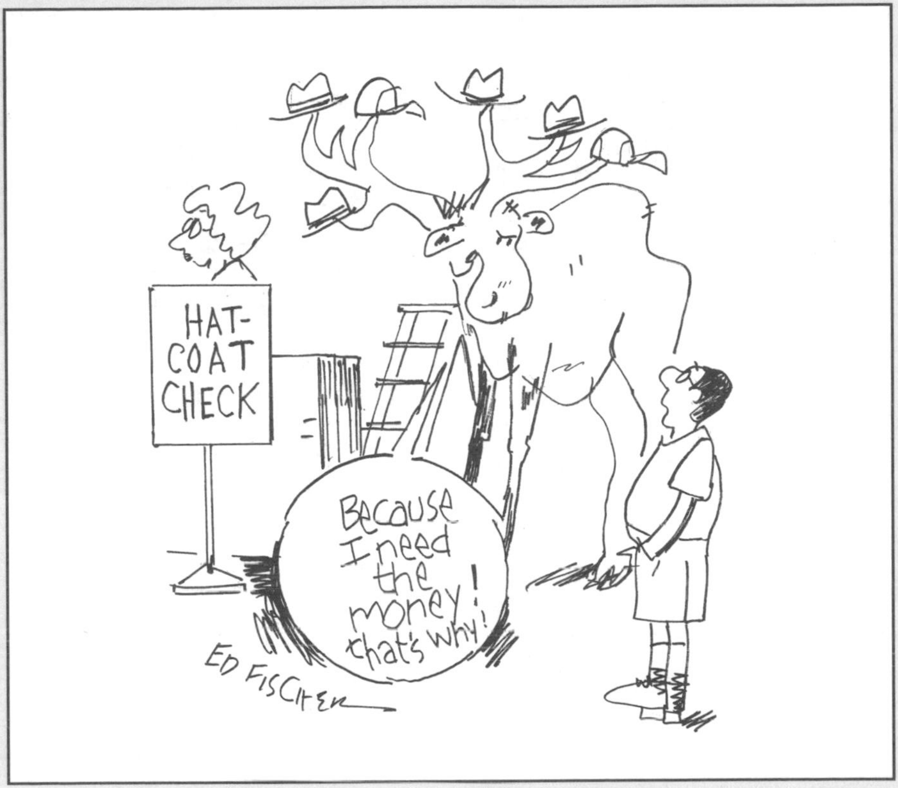
HAT-
COAT
CHECK
Because I need the money! that's why!
ED FISCHER

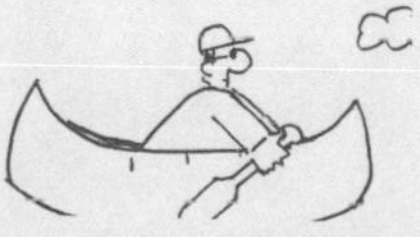

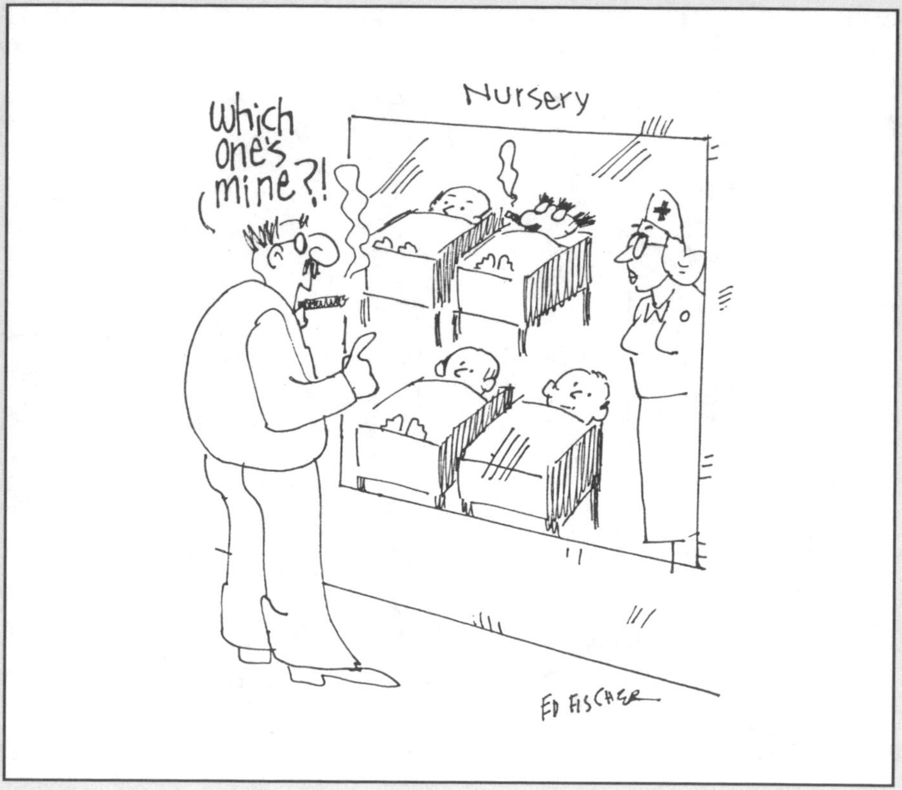
Which one's mine?!
Nursery
ED FISCHER

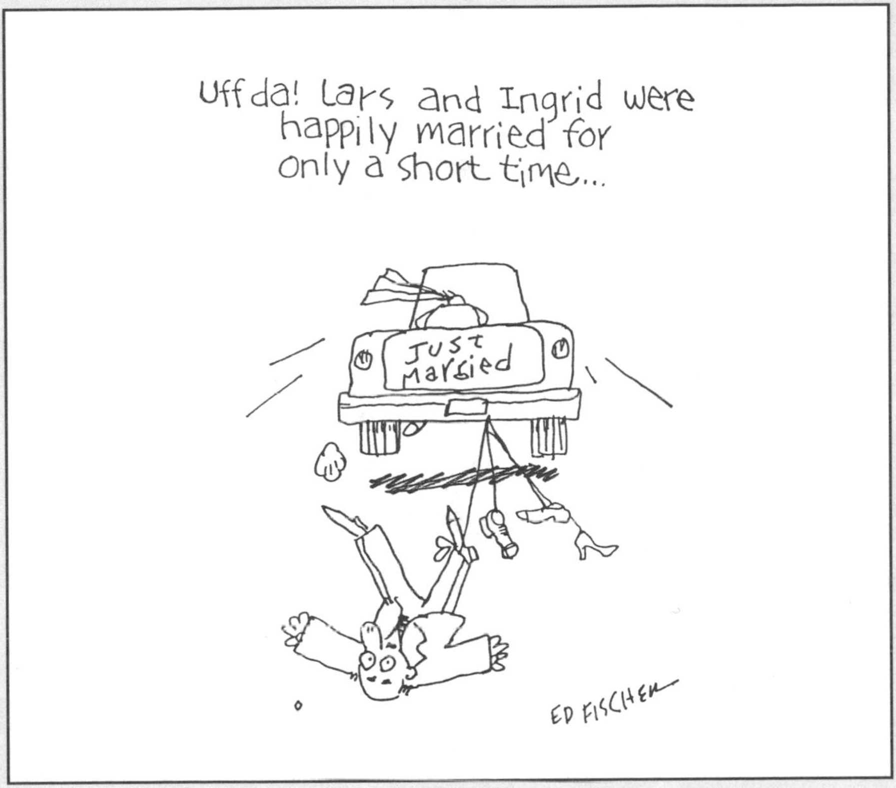
Uff da! Lars and Ingrid were happily married for only a short time...
JUST Married
ED FISCHER

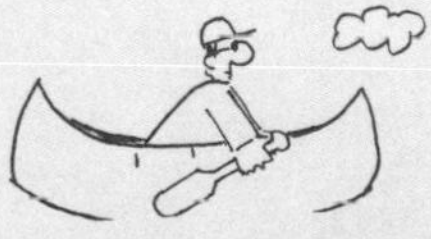

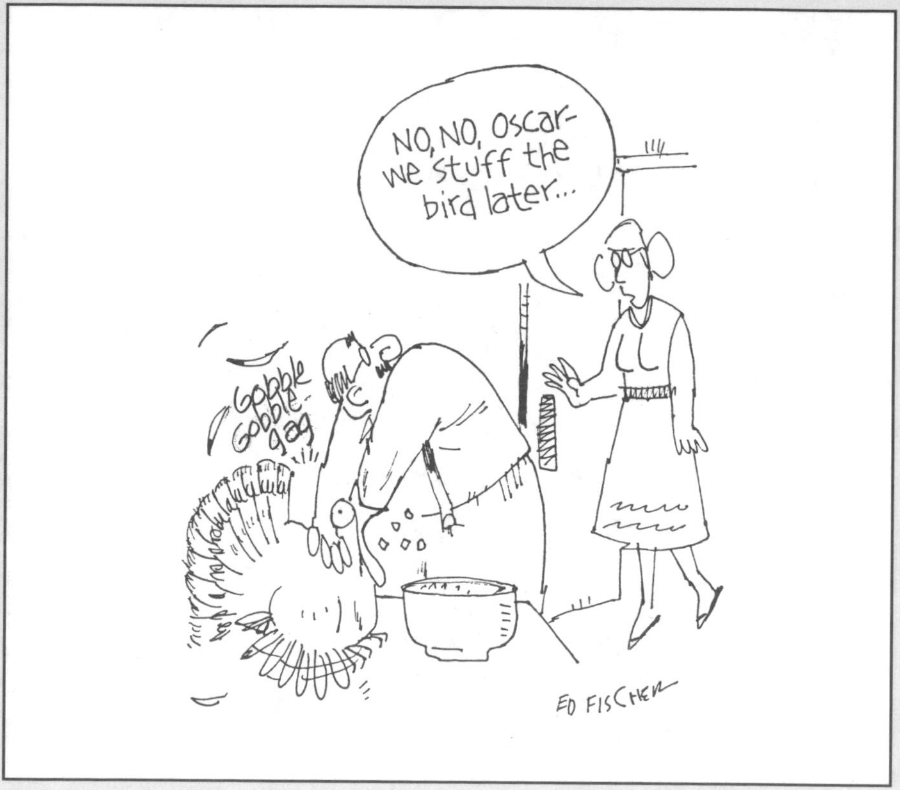
NO, NO, OSCAR-
we stuff the
bird later...
Gobble
Gobble
gag
ED FISCHER

Two old friends, Mike and Oscar, were done hiking and decided to bed down for the night. Exhausted from hiking, they quickly fell asleep but woke later to see a sky filled with stars.

"Wow" says Mike. "Look at those stars. Aren't they magnificent?"

Oscar says, "What does that mean to you, Mike?"

"Well," says Mike, "I think it means we are all but small bits in a giant universe created by a loving God. What does it mean to you, Oscar?"

"I think it means someone stole our tent."

The only time a fisherman tells the truth is when he calls another fisherman a liar.

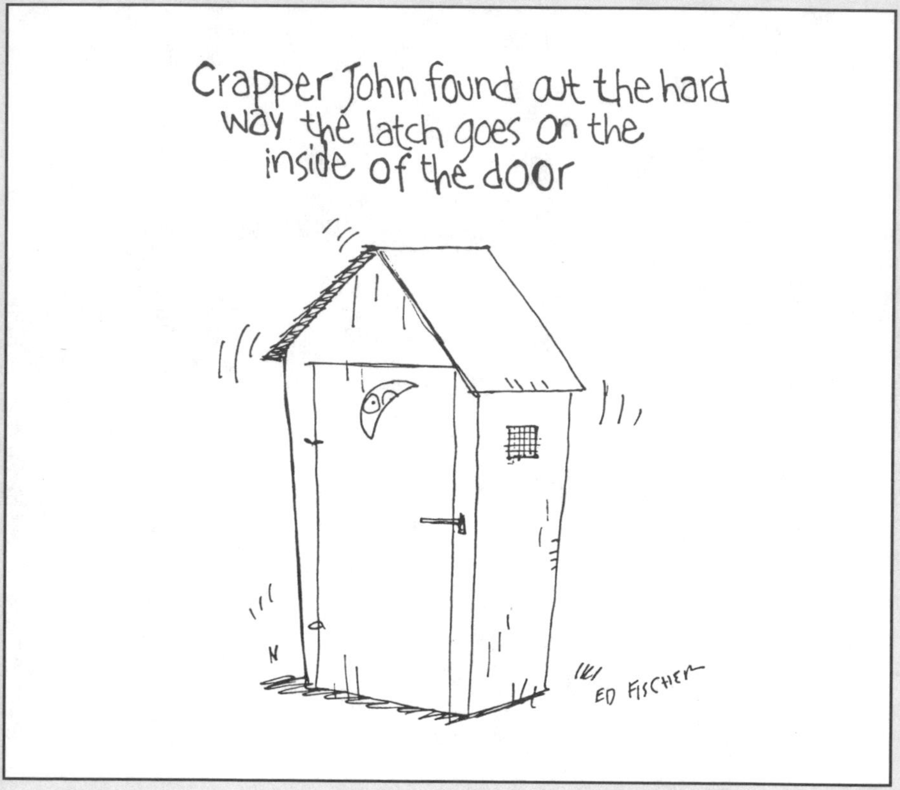
Crapper John found out the hard way the latch goes on the inside of the door
ED FISCHER

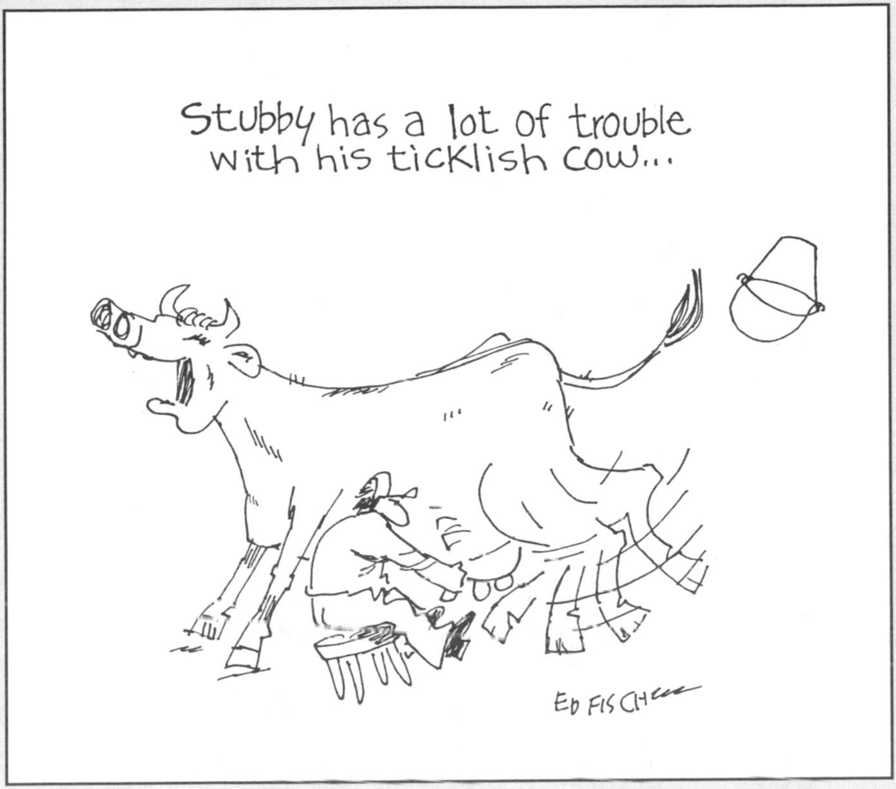
Stubby has a lot of trouble with his ticklish cow...

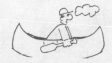

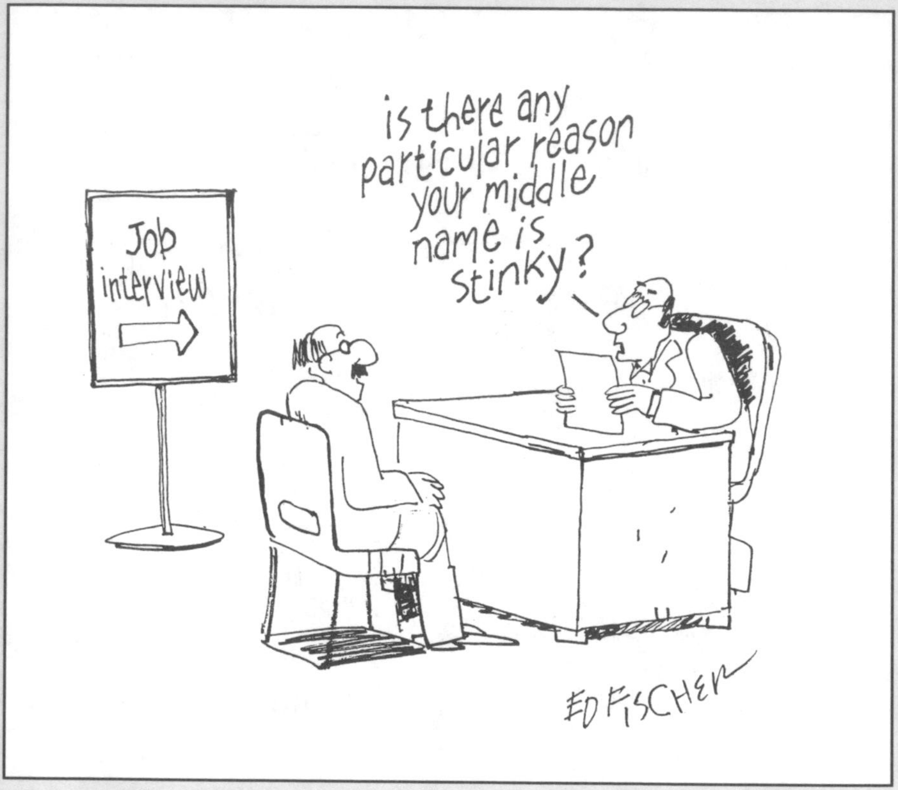
is there any particular reason your middle name is stinky?
Job interview
ED FISCHER

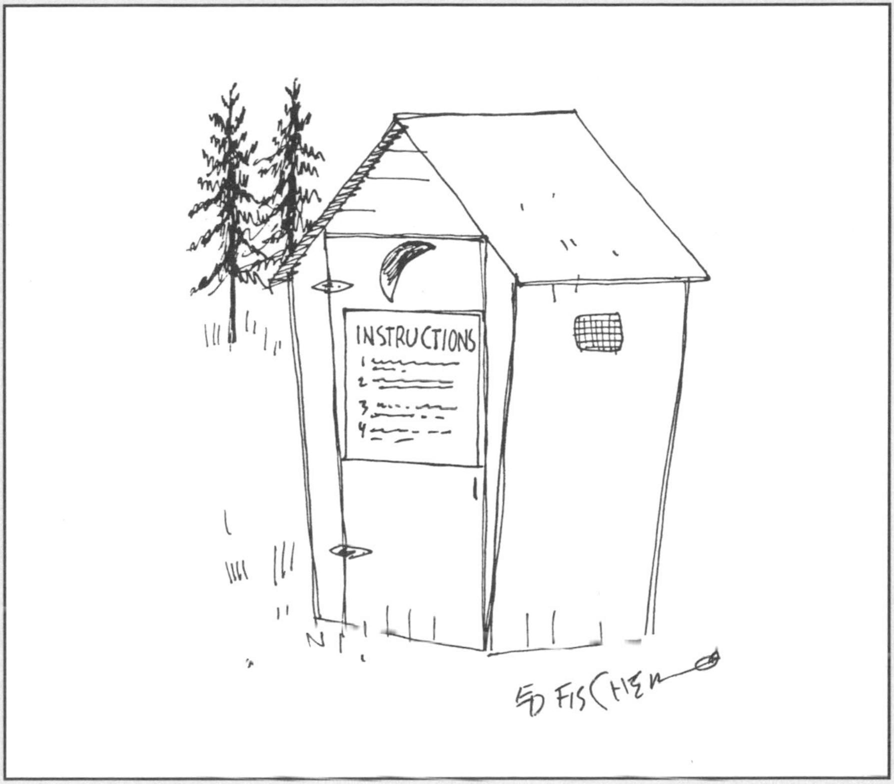
INSTRUCTIONS
1
2
3
4
ED FISCHER

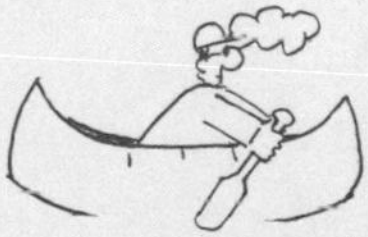

A fisherman in a small boat sees another man in a small boat take a mirror out of his tackle box and shine it into the water. Curious, he asks what the mirror is for. The other man says, "This is how I catch fish. I shine the light into the water and when the fish come up to the top I nab them."

"Does it really work?" he asks.

"You bet it does. It's a very special mirror!"

"I'll give you ten bucks for that mirror," the fisherman says.

"Okay."

"By the way, how many have you caught?"

"You're the sixth one this week."

A man returns from a weekend fishing trip and is upset with his wife. "Why didn't you pack my warm pajamas!?"

The wife says, "I did. I put them in your tackle box."

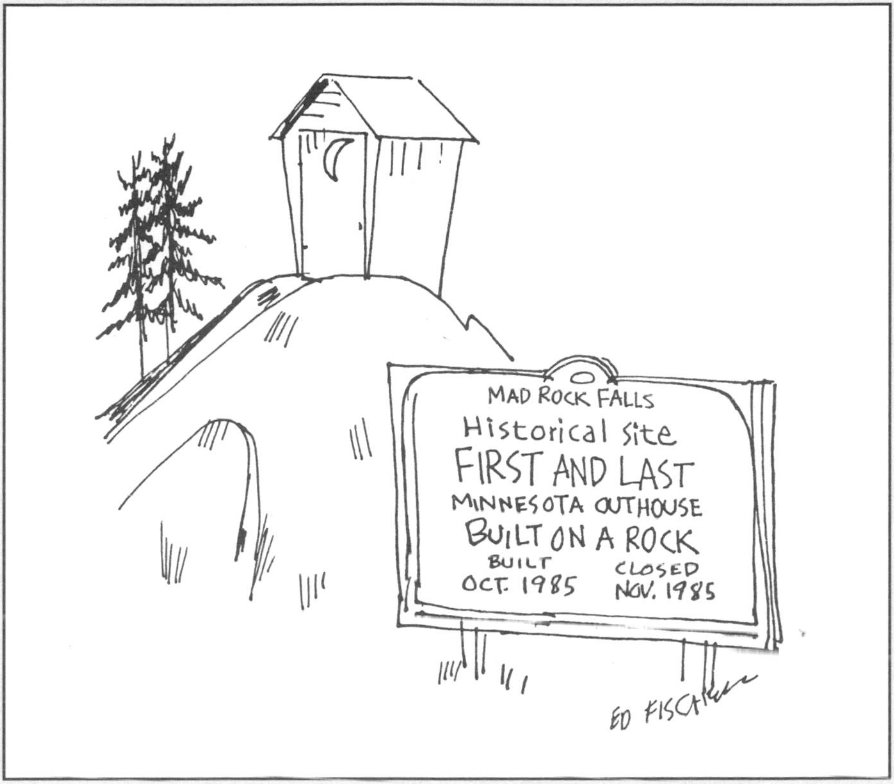
MAD ROCK FALLS
Historical site
FIRST AND LAST
MINNESOTA OUTHOUSE
BUILT ON A ROCK
BUILT
OCT. 1985
CLOSED
NOV. 1985
ED FISCHER

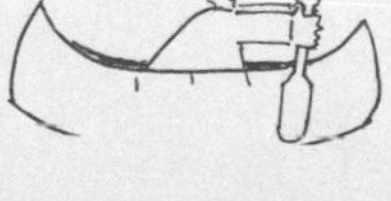

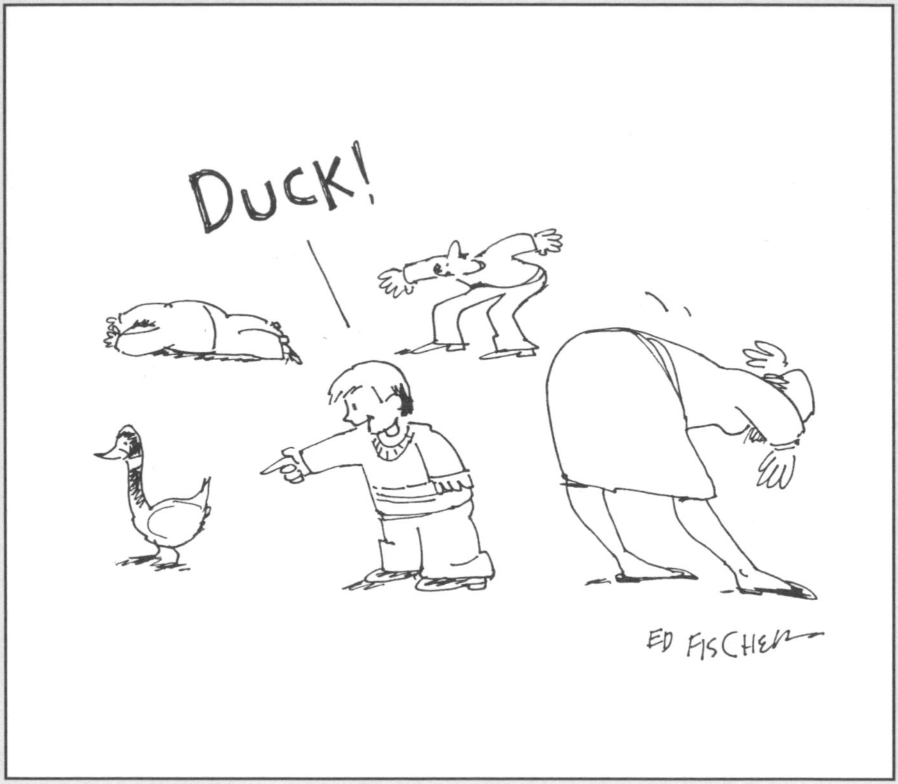
DUCK!
ED FISCHER

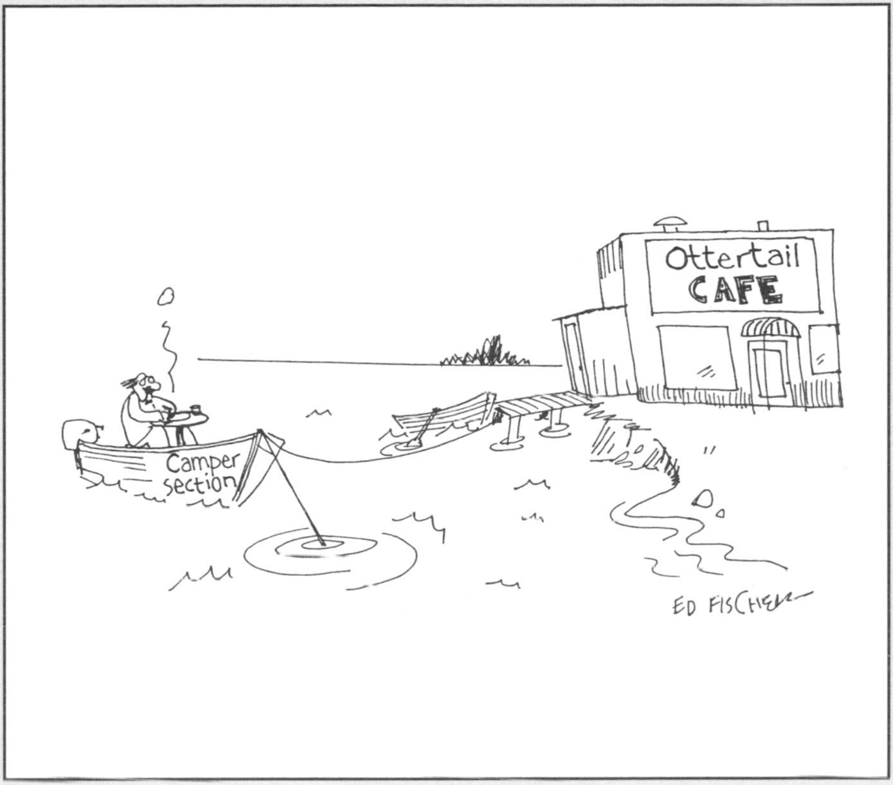
Ottertail
CAFE
Camper
section
ED FISCHER

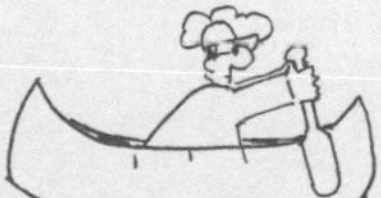

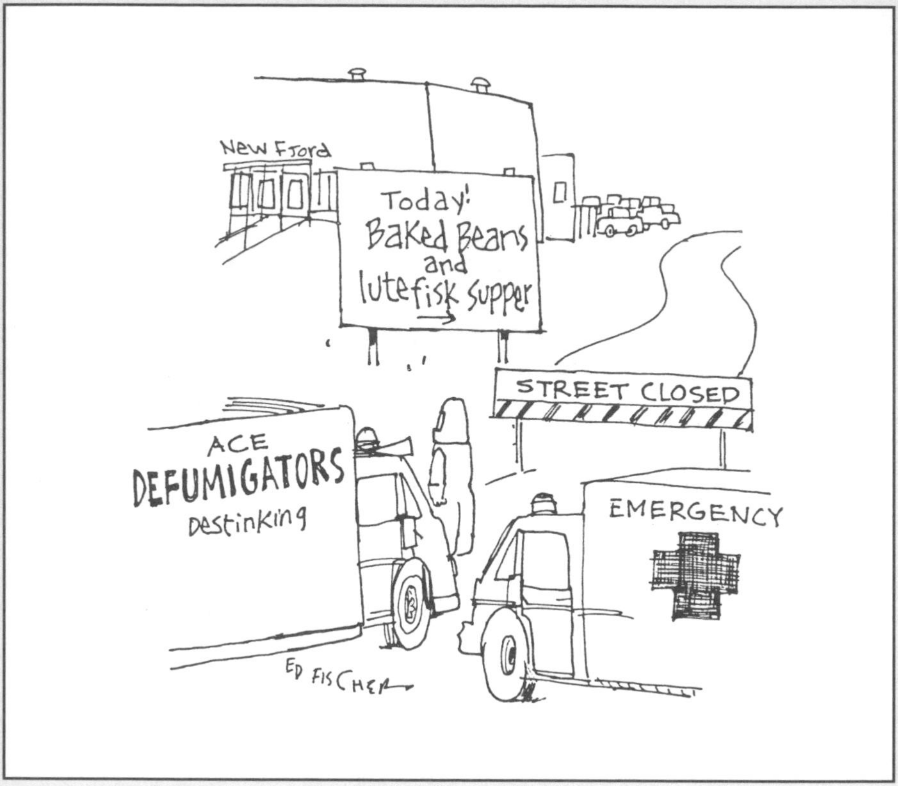
New Fjord
Today!
Baked Beans
and
lutefisk supper
STREET CLOSED
ACE
DEFUMIGATORS
Destinking
EMERGENCY
ED FISCHER

Sparky invented coffee that makes you see double. It keeps you up at night, but you have company.

Two grumpy old hunters up in northern Minnesota come across some tracks. One says "I recognize these tracks... as sure as I'm standing here, these are bear tracks!"

"You're crazy?" says the grumpy old man. "Anybody knows these are deer tracks! Look here!"

They stood for quite a while yelling back and forth, moving the snow around with their feet. Then, as they bent over to look closer, both were run over by a train.

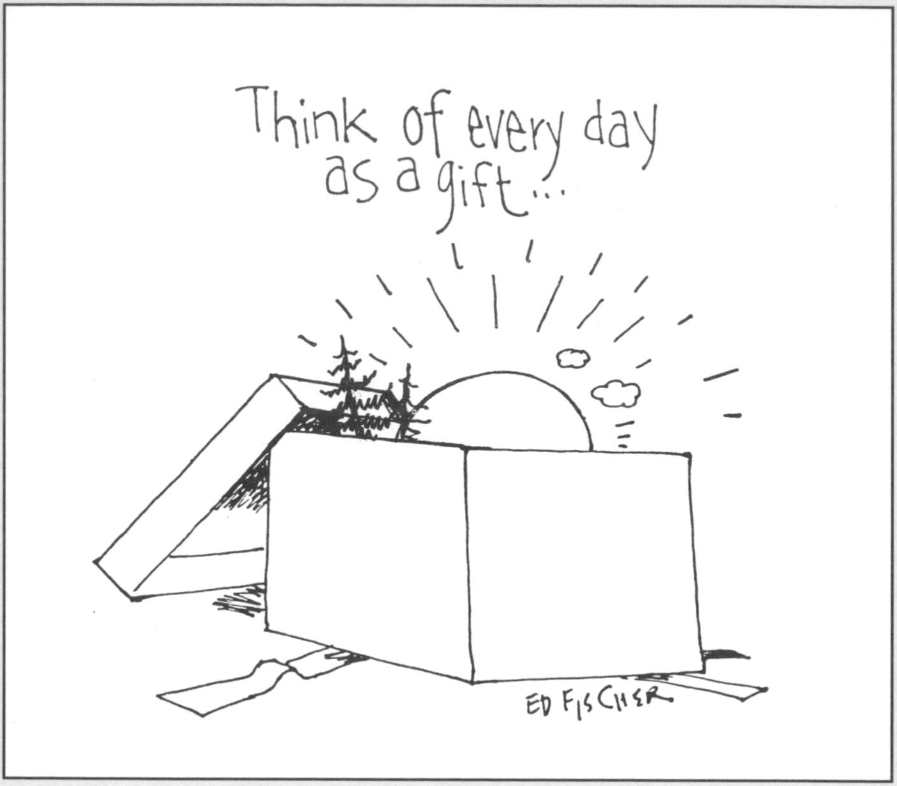
Think of every day
as a gift...
ED FISCHER

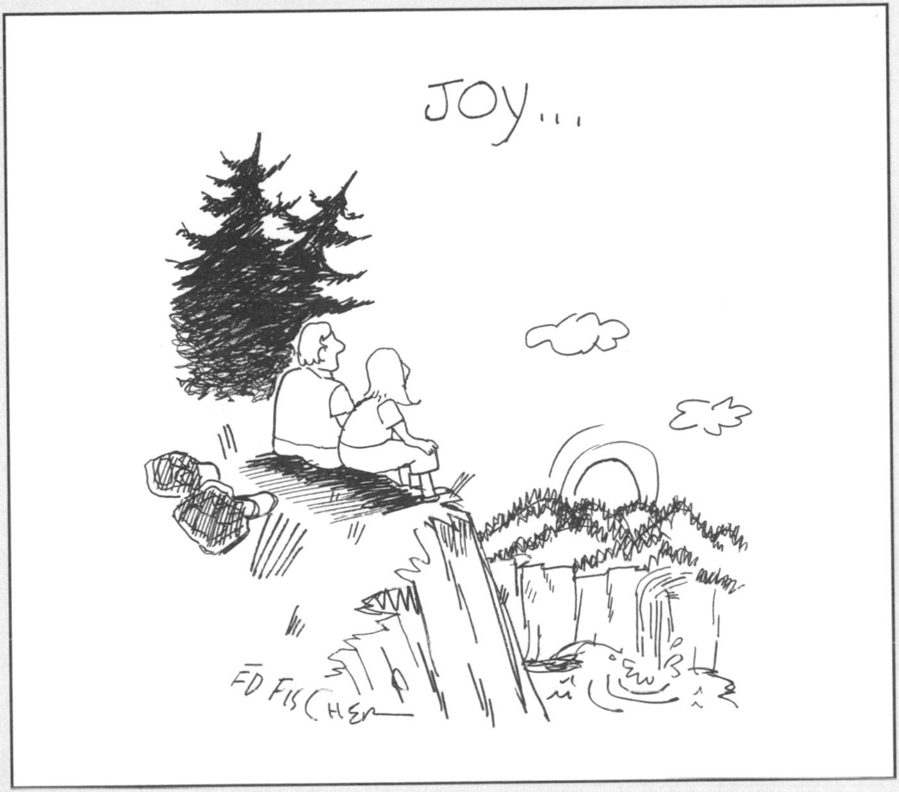
JOY...
ED FISCHER

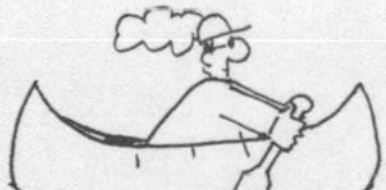

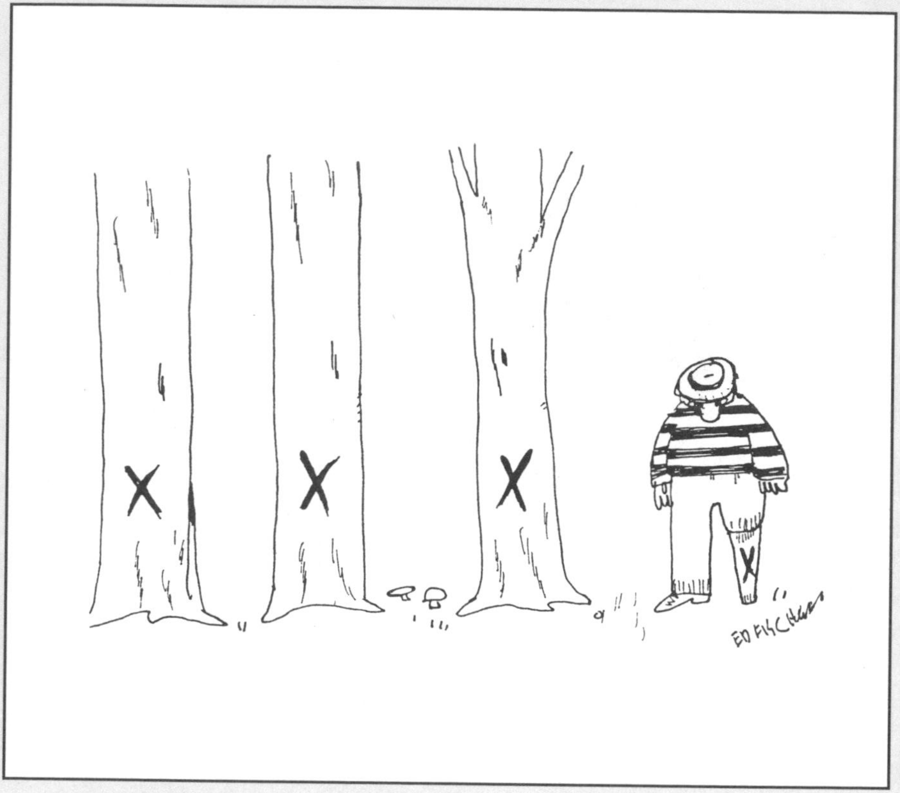

The Northwoods Camp counselor called Moosey and said that Moosey Jr. was sleeping with a stray dog.

"But what about the smell?" Moosey asked.

"The dog's getting used to it," the counselor replied.

A woman goes fishing with her husband. After an hour, she asks, "Do you have any more of those little round plastic floaty things? Mine keep sinking."

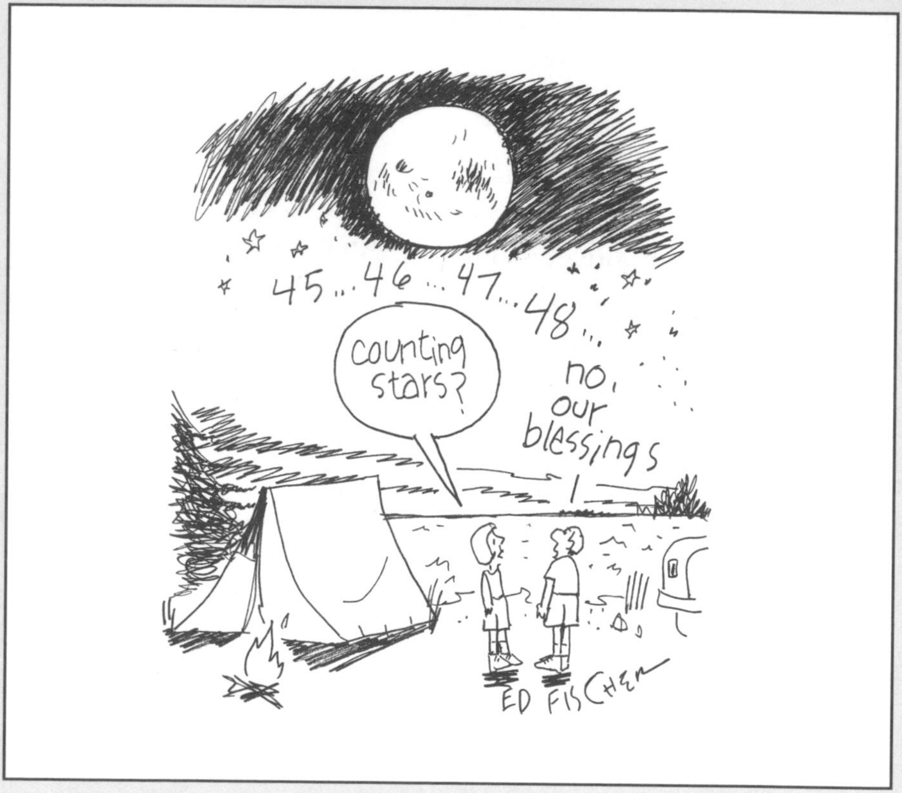
45...46...47...48...
counting stars?
no, our blessings
ED FISCHER

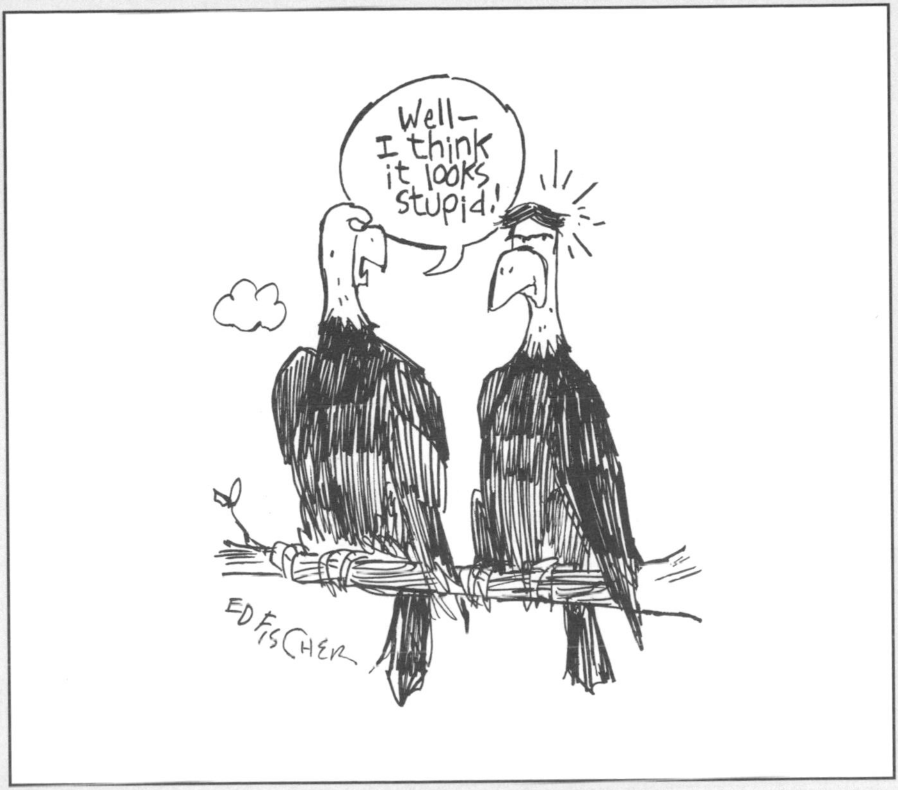
Well—
I think
it looks
stupid!
ED FISCHER

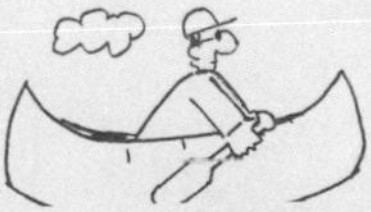

A neighbor of Rusty's named Tates decided to become a rich entrepreneur. Out hiking one day he noticed all the hikers and decided he would make a better, less expensive compass. Amid a fanfare of national publicity he launched his cheaper compass. At first he was a big success, but as thousands of people got lost with his inferior compass, he received a lot of bad publicity. His empire collapsed when *Newsweek* magazine carried the headline: "He Who Has a Tates is Lost."

What's the difference between unlawful and illegal? Unlawful is against the law, illegal is a sick bird.

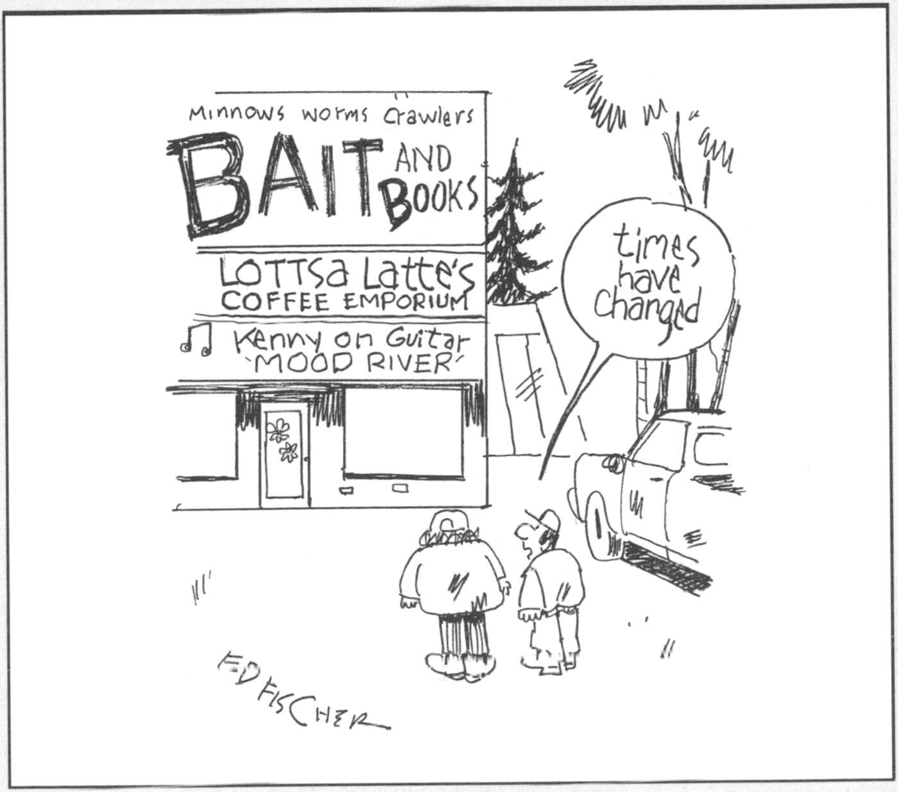
Minnows worms crawlers
BAIT AND BOOKS
LOTTSa Latte's
COFFEE EMPORIUM
Kenny on Guitar
'MOOD RIVER'
times have changed
ED FISCHER

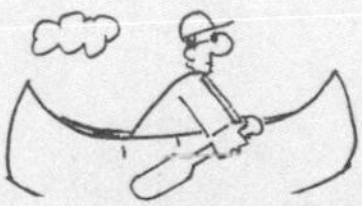

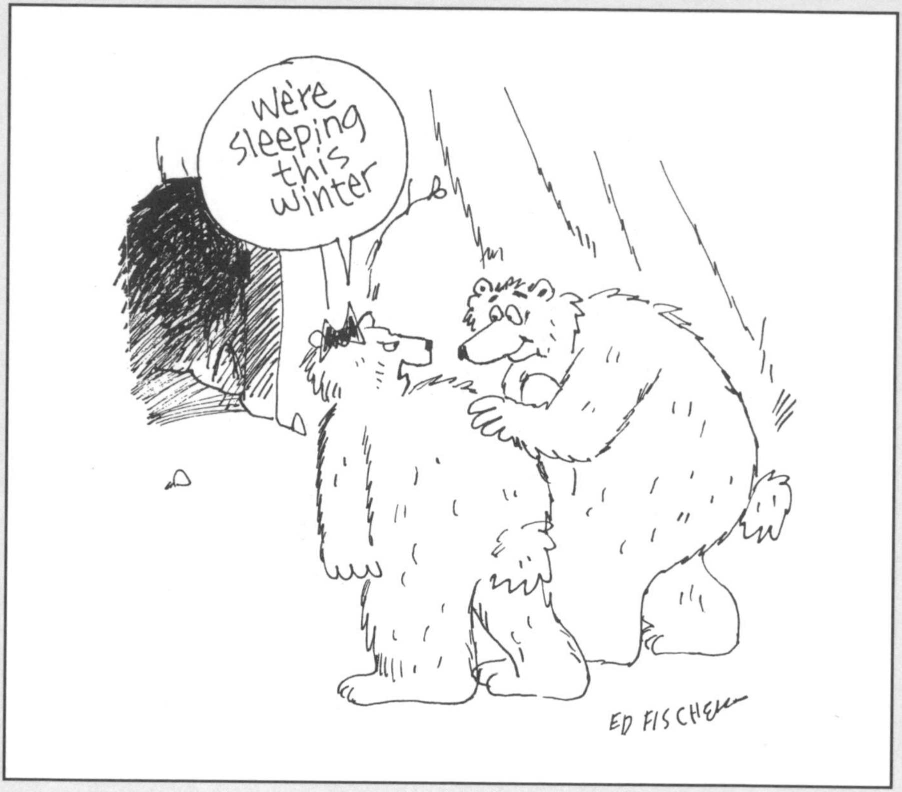
We're sleeping this winter
ED FISCHER

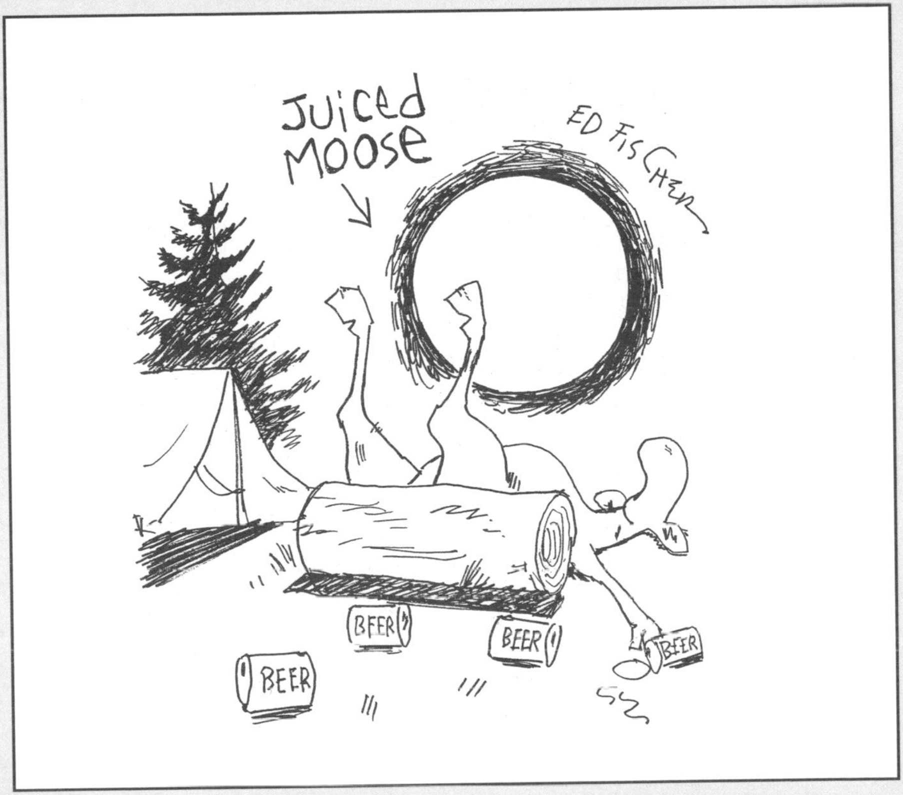
Juiced Moose
ED FISCHER
BEER
BEER
BEER
BEER

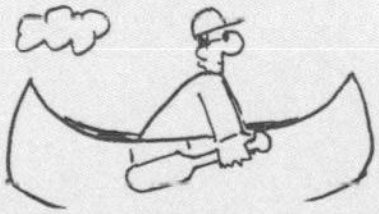

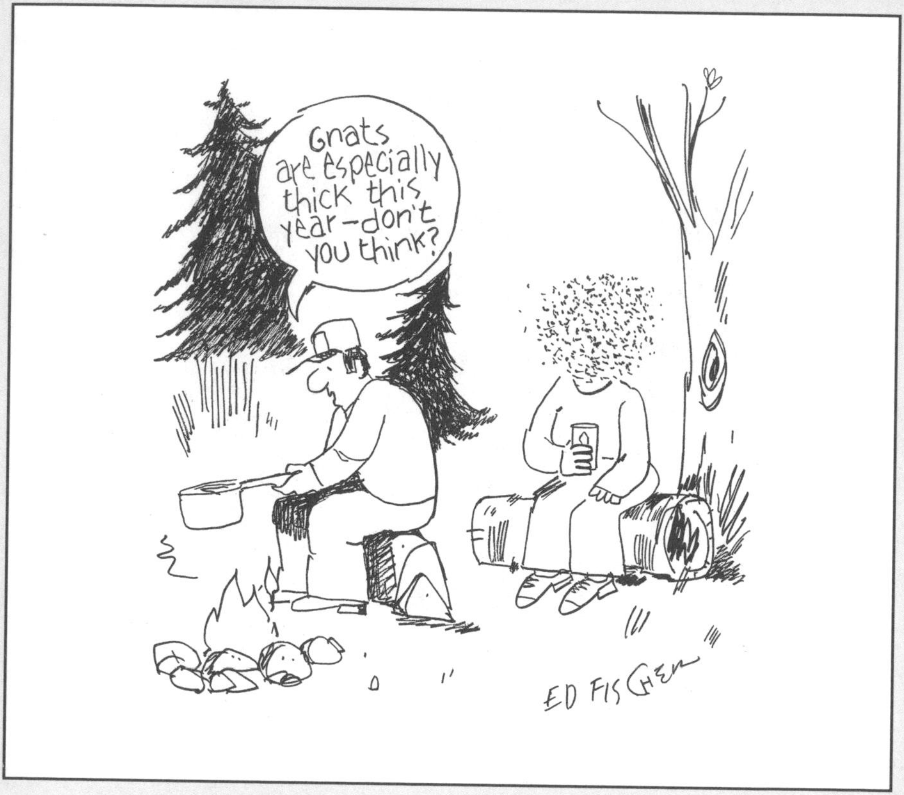
Gnats are especially thick this year-don't you think?
ED FISCHER

Coffee can be bad for you. Sparky knows someone who went blind drinking coffee. She kept leaving the spoon in the cup.

There isn't much to do in Owl's Head Junction. Every Saturday night many of the townspeople go down to the train to see people off... and the train doesn't stop in Owl's Head!

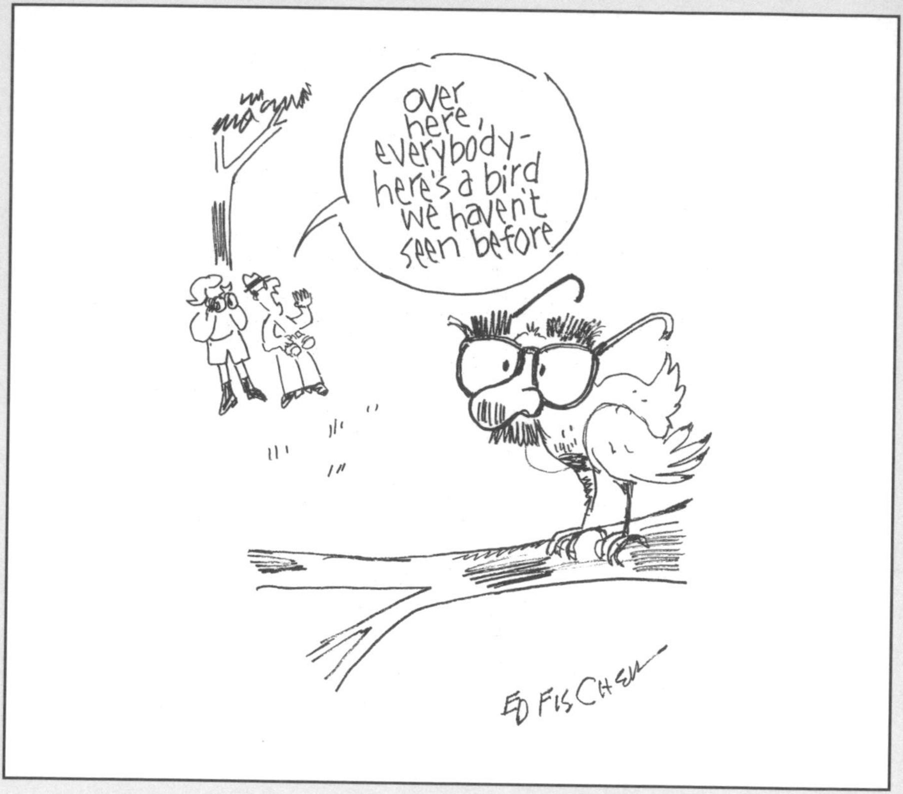
over here, everybody- here's a bird we haven't seen before
ED FISCHER

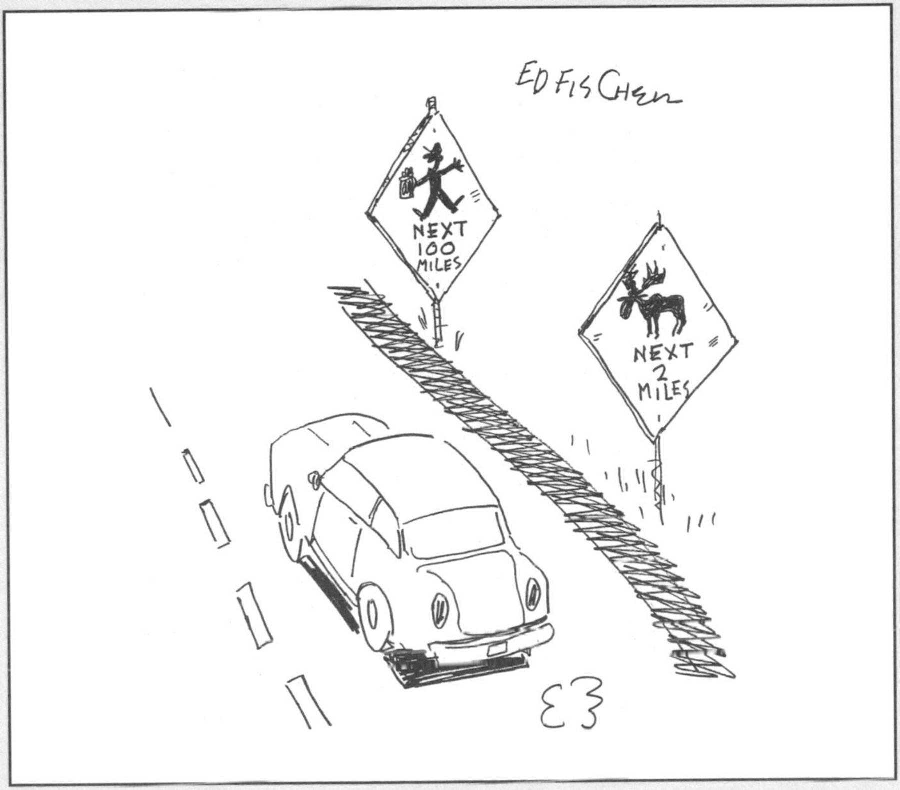
ED FISCHER
NEXT
100
MILES
NEXT
2
MILES

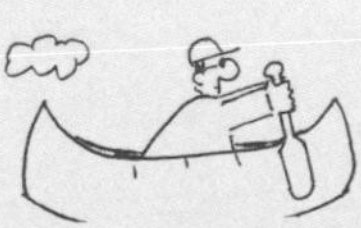

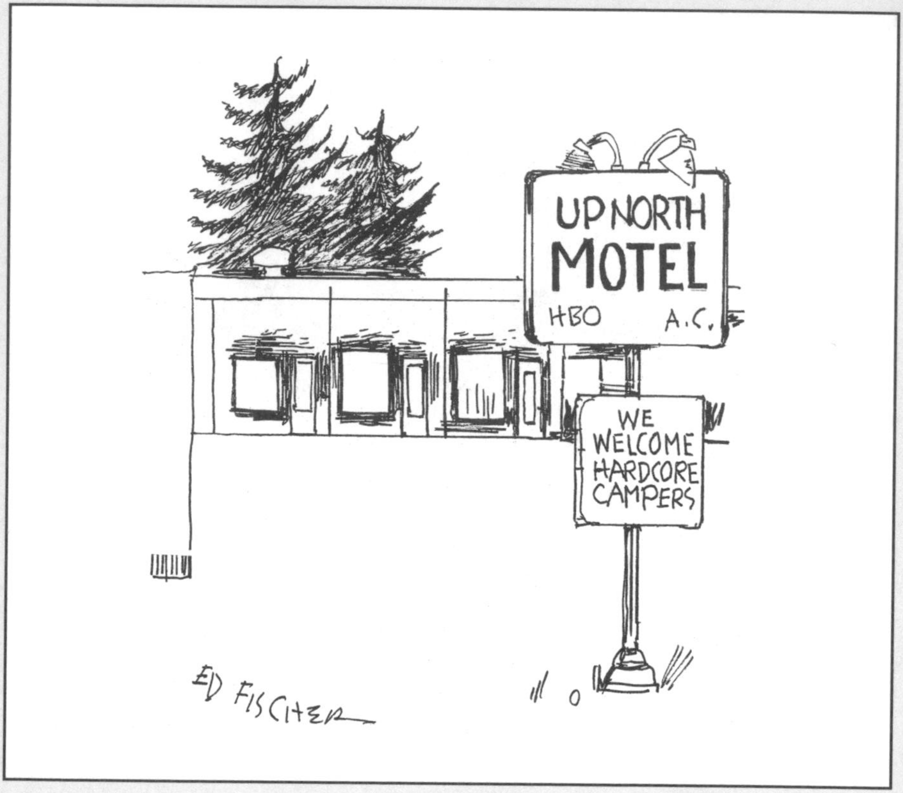
UP NORTH
MOTEL
HBO A.C.
WE
WELCOME
HARDCORE
CAMPERS
ED FISCHER

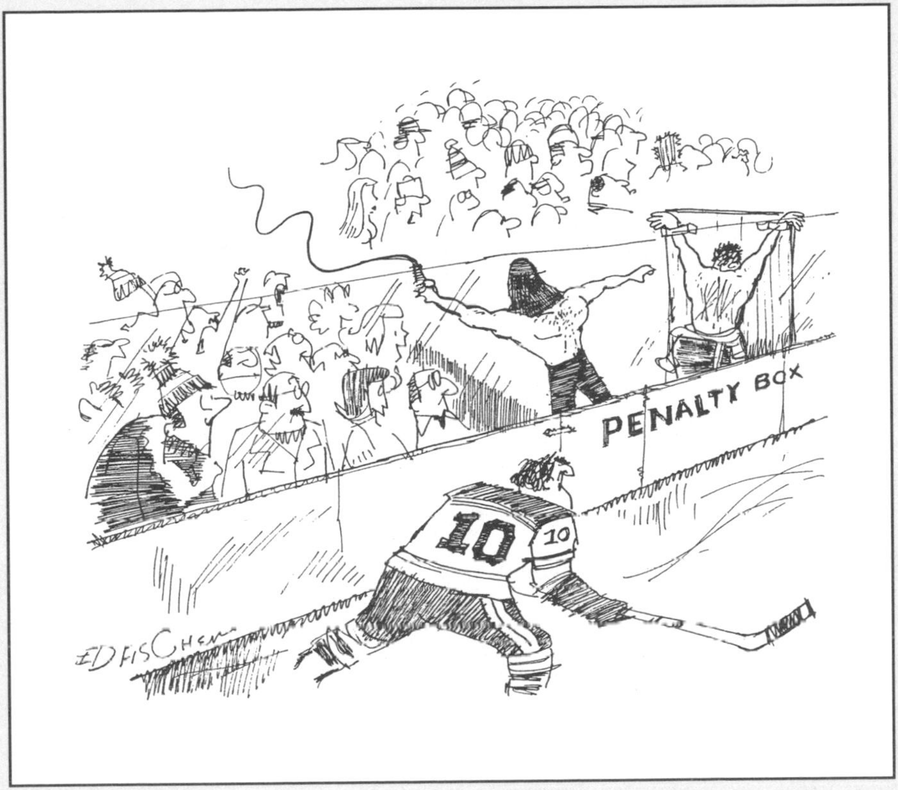
PENALTY BOX
10
10

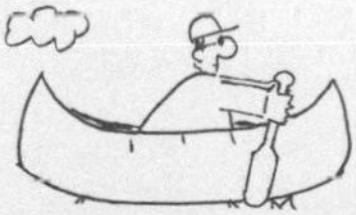

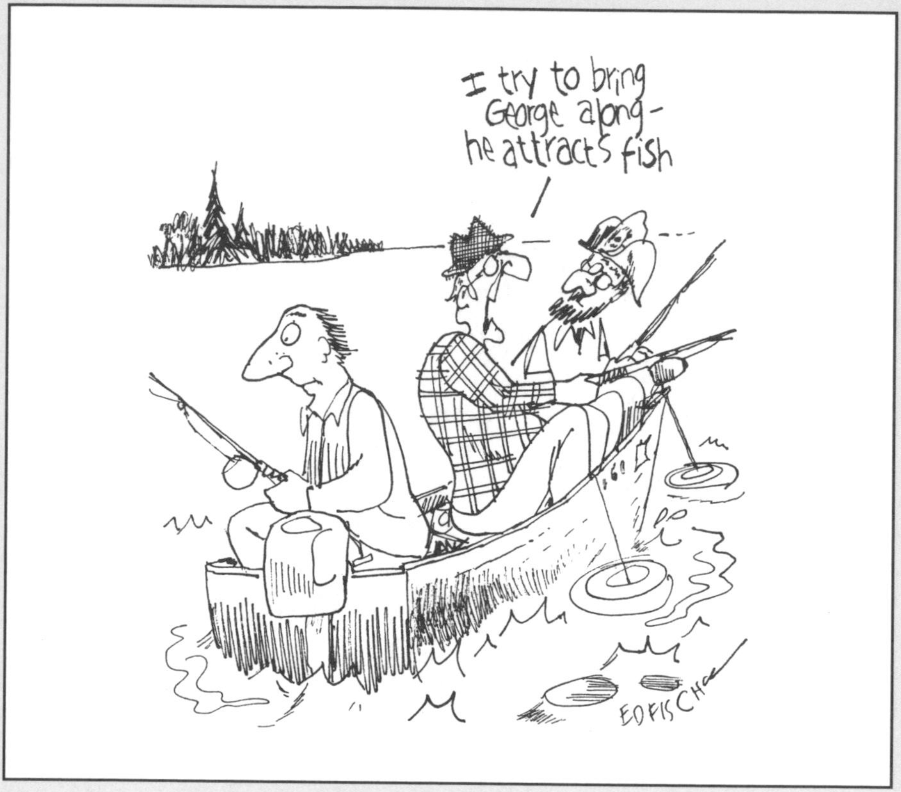
I try to bring George along - he attracts fish
EDFISCHER

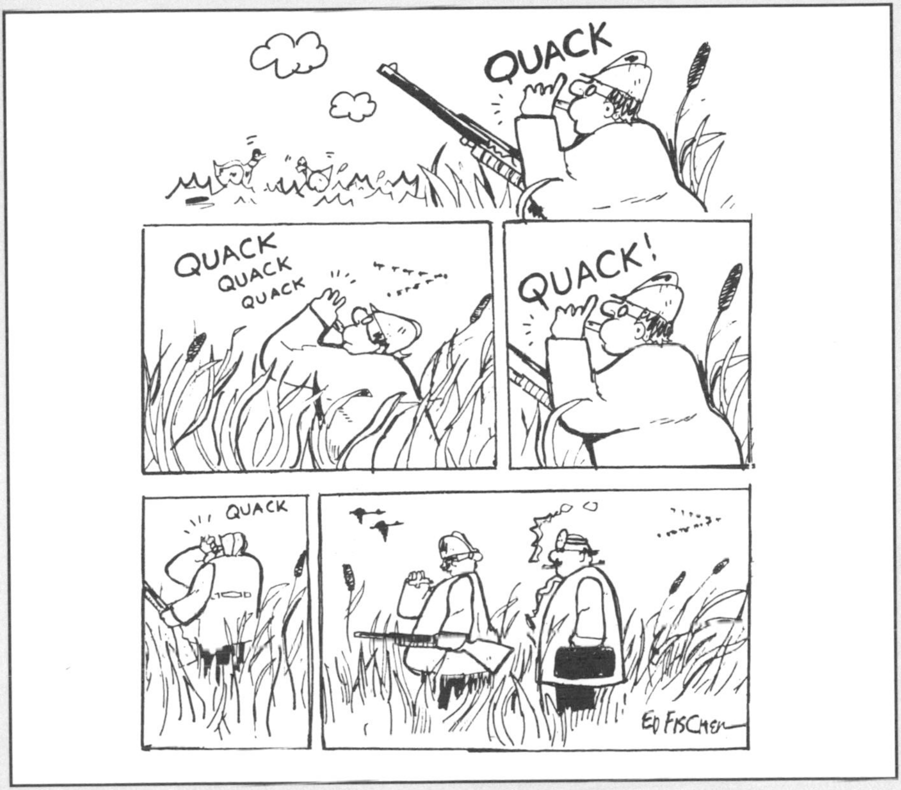
QUACK
QUACK
QUACK
QUACK
QUACK!
QUACK
ED FISCHER

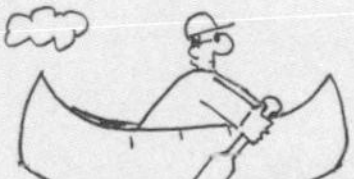

George and Oscar go on a fishing trip. The first day, George catches his limit. Oscar gets nothing. Oscar can't understand it. He's a better fisherman. It's just luck. The second day George catches one right after the other. He catches his limit and Oscar is skunked again. Oscar is fuming.

The next day Oscar gets up early and, without George, goes to the very spot they were fishing the day before and drops his line in the water. He feels a tug, reels it in and all that's on the line is a note. It says, "Where's George?"

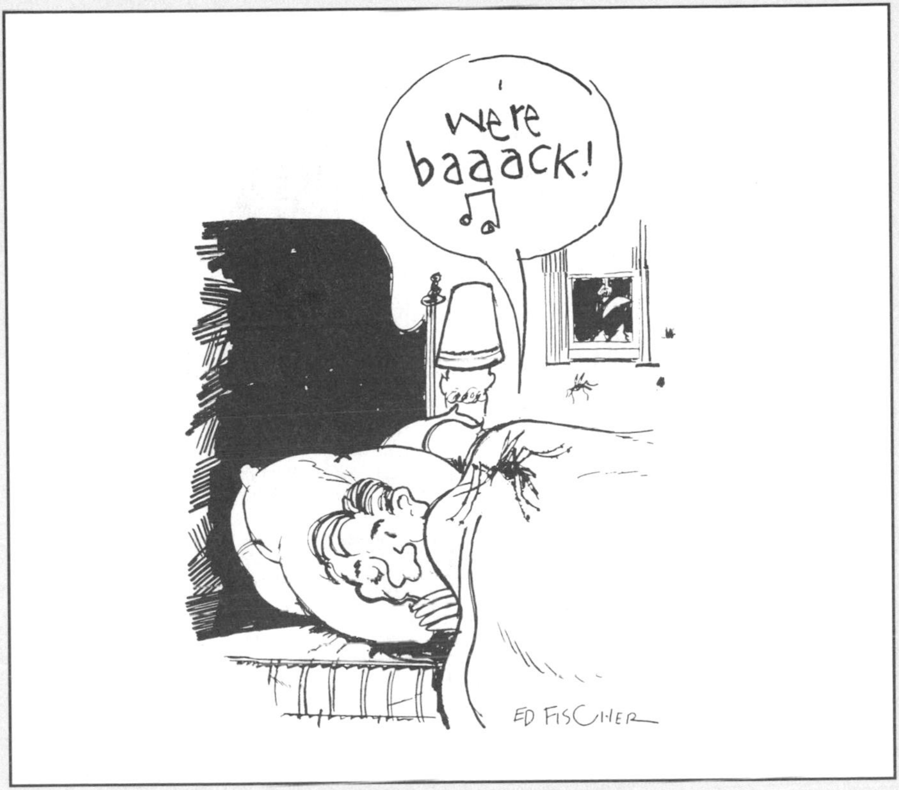
we're baaack!
ED FISCHER

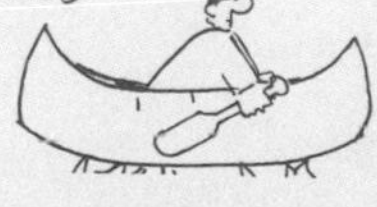

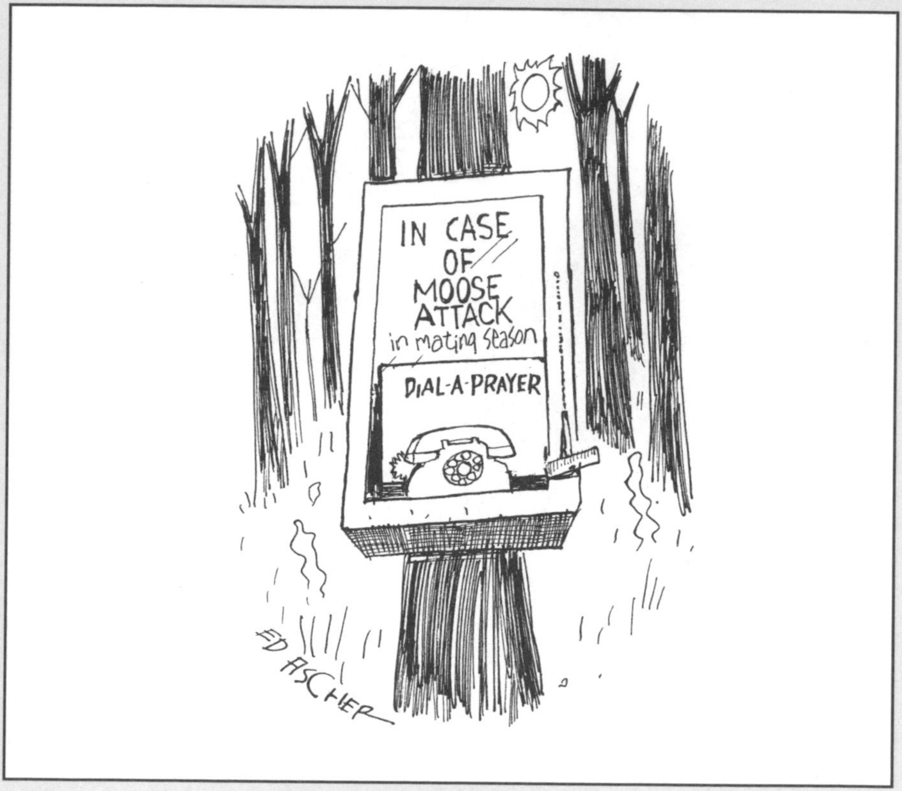
IN CASE OF MOOSE ATTACK
in mating season
DIAL-A-PRAYER
ED ASCHER

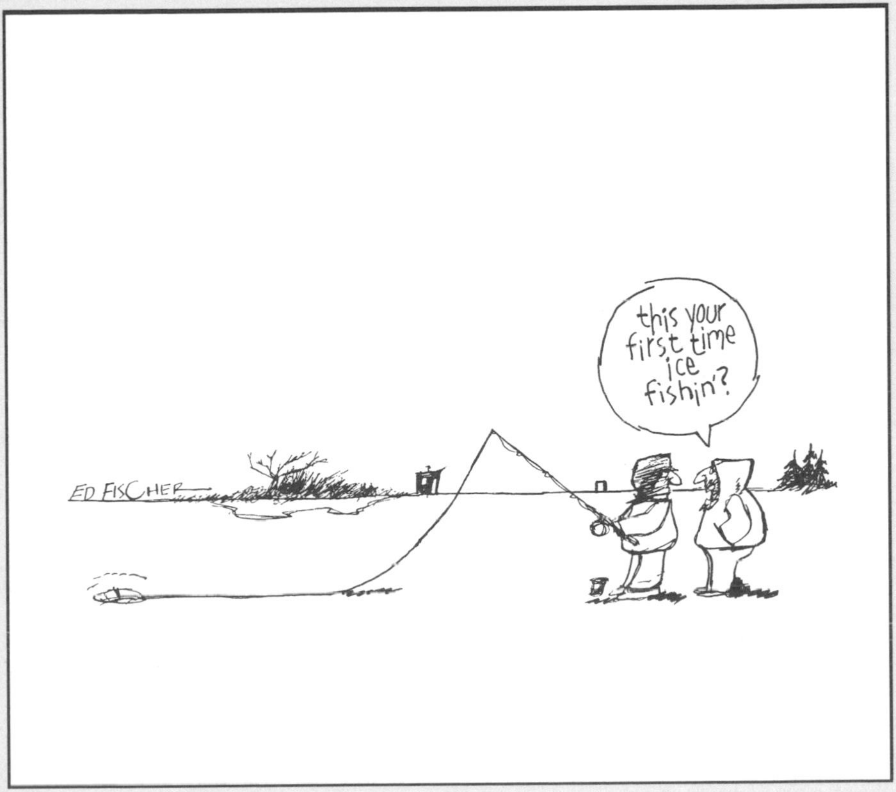
this your first time ice fishin'?
ED FISCHER

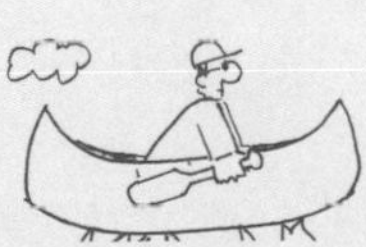

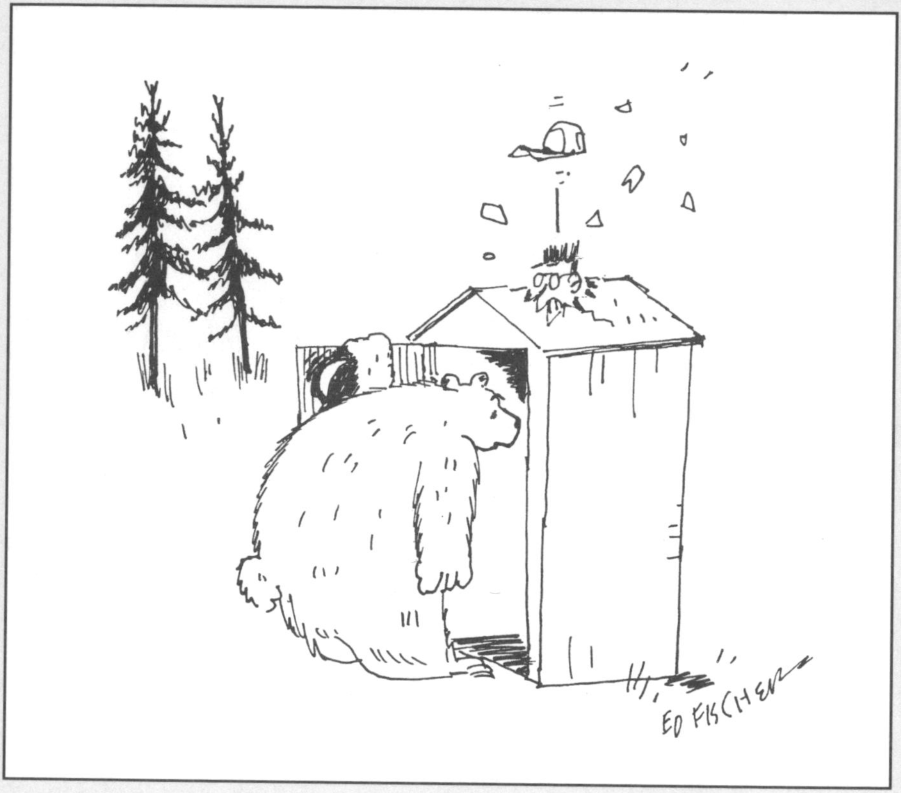
ED FISCHER

Lars and Ingrid happened to be at the New Fjord airport when a pilot offered them a joyride—under one condition.

"This is a real fun ride," he said. "And I have my fun this way: if you don't make one sound from all the loop-the-loops, I'll charge you only $25. But if I hear one scream or any sound, I'll charge you $100."

So up they went, doing all these crazy stunts. They came back down and the pilot was amazed. They hadn't uttered one word.

The pilot said to Lars, "That's amazing. You didn't say a word!"

"Almost did, though," Lars said, "when Ingrid fell out."

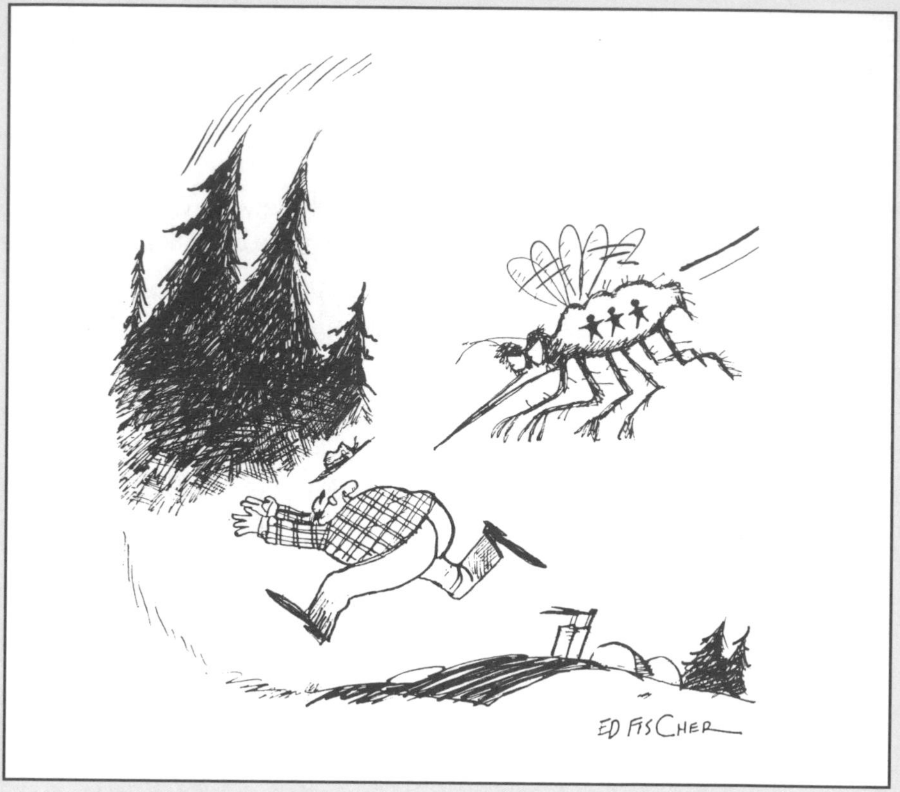
ED FISCHER

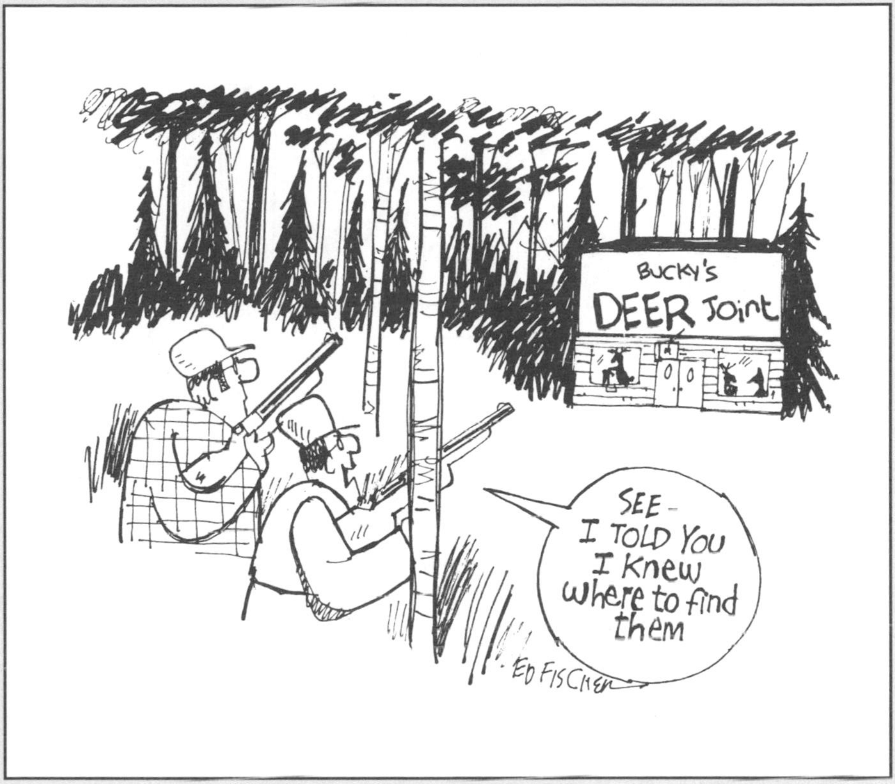
BUCKY'S
DEER Joint
SEE - I TOLD YOU I Knew where to find them
ED FISCHER

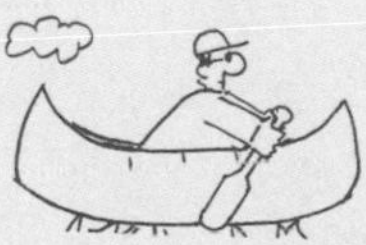

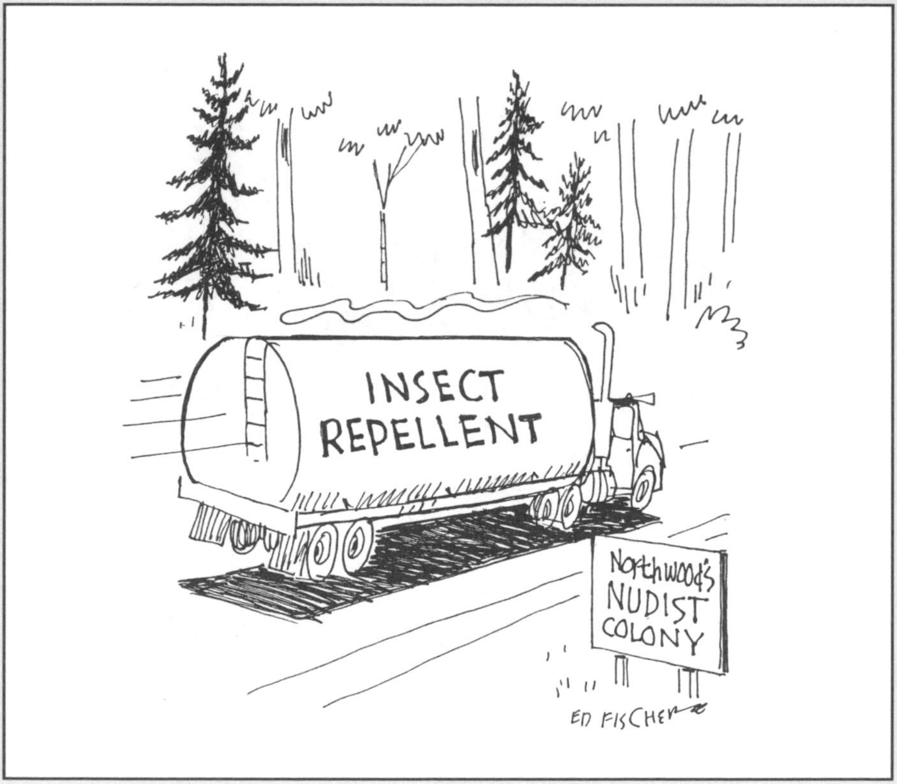
INSECT REPELLENT
Northwood's NUDIST COLONY
ED FISCHER

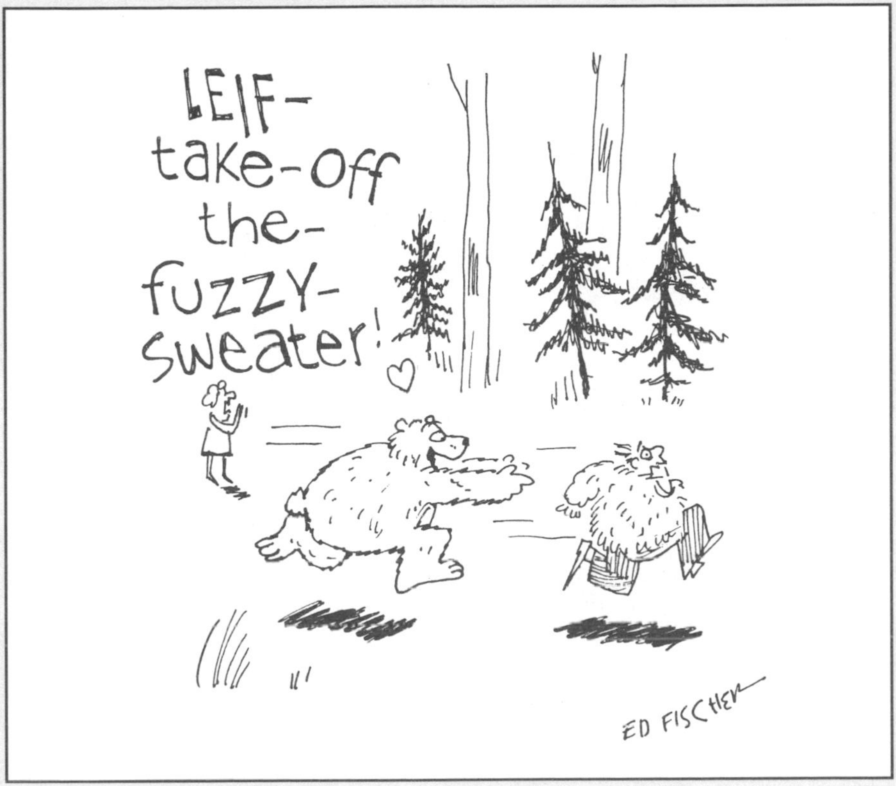
LEIF-
take-off
the-
fuzzy-
sweater!
ED FISCHER

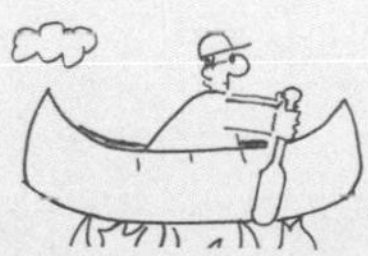

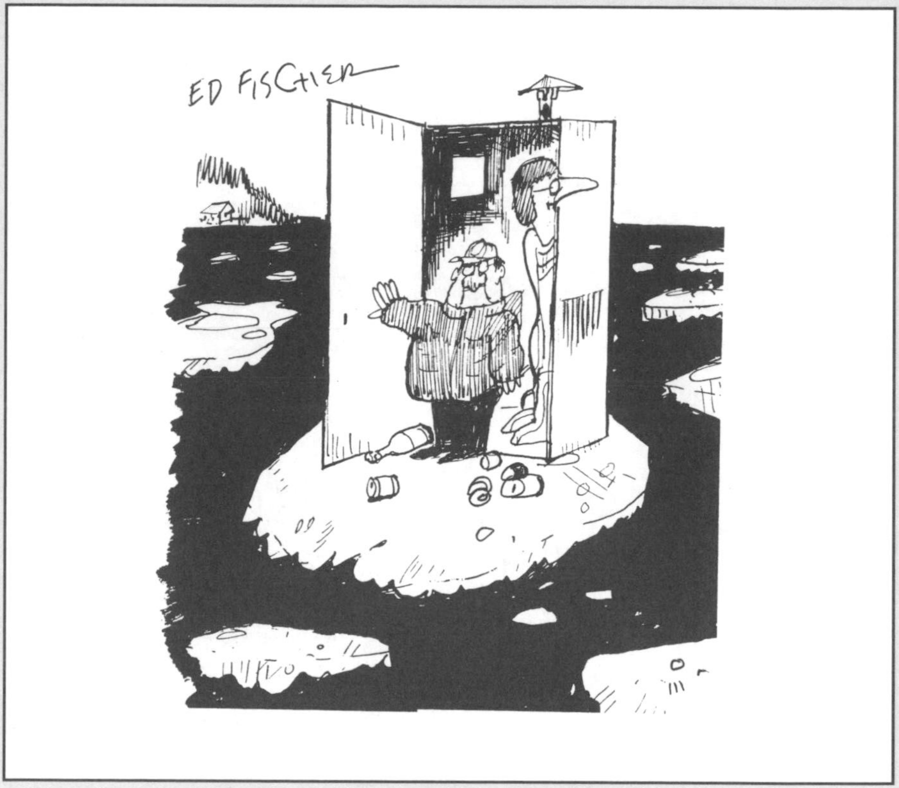
ED FISCHER

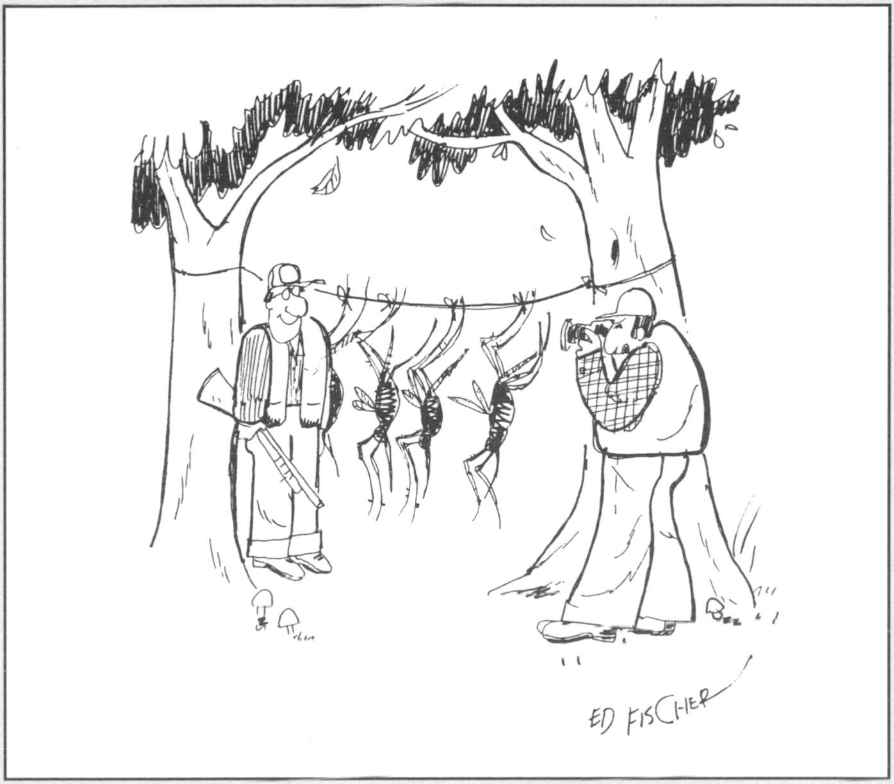
ED FISCHER

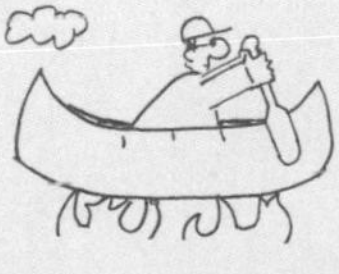

Two hunters way up north, in Canada, bag a moose each. When they return to the plane that is going to fly them out, the pilot says, "I can't take those moose on the plane. They are much too heavy!"

"C'mon," says one the hunters. "We flew two just like these out of here last year!"

"Okay," says the pilot.

They load them up and take off. Seconds later they crash into the woods. "Isn't this something?" says the other hunter. "This is almost exactly where we crashed last year."

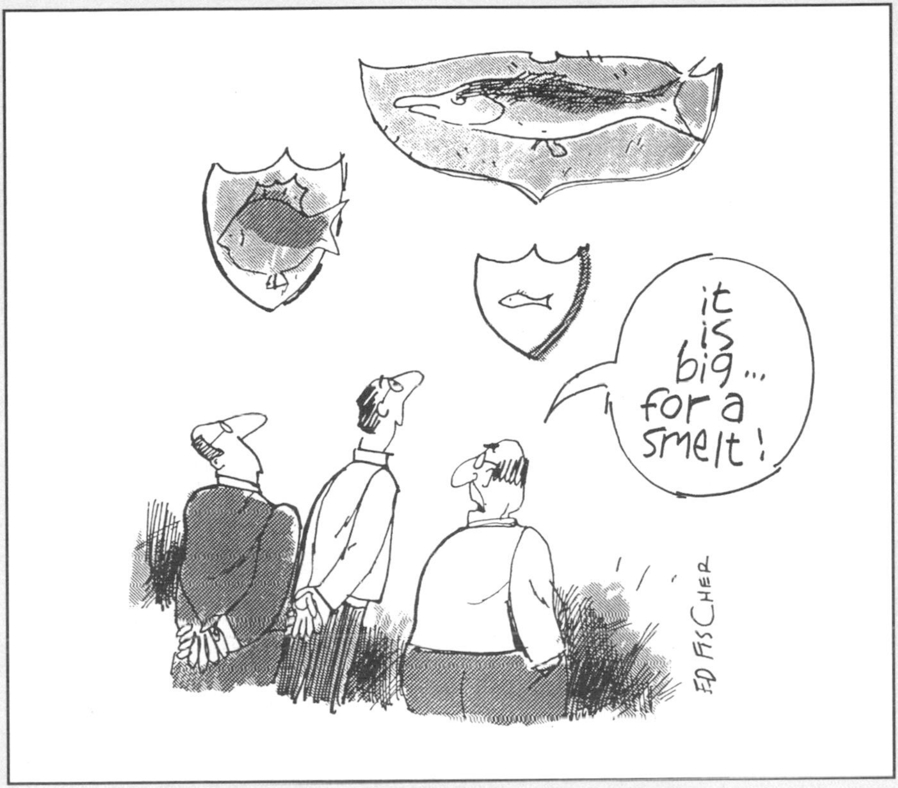
it is big... for a smelt!
ED FISCHER

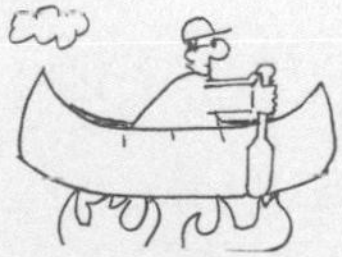

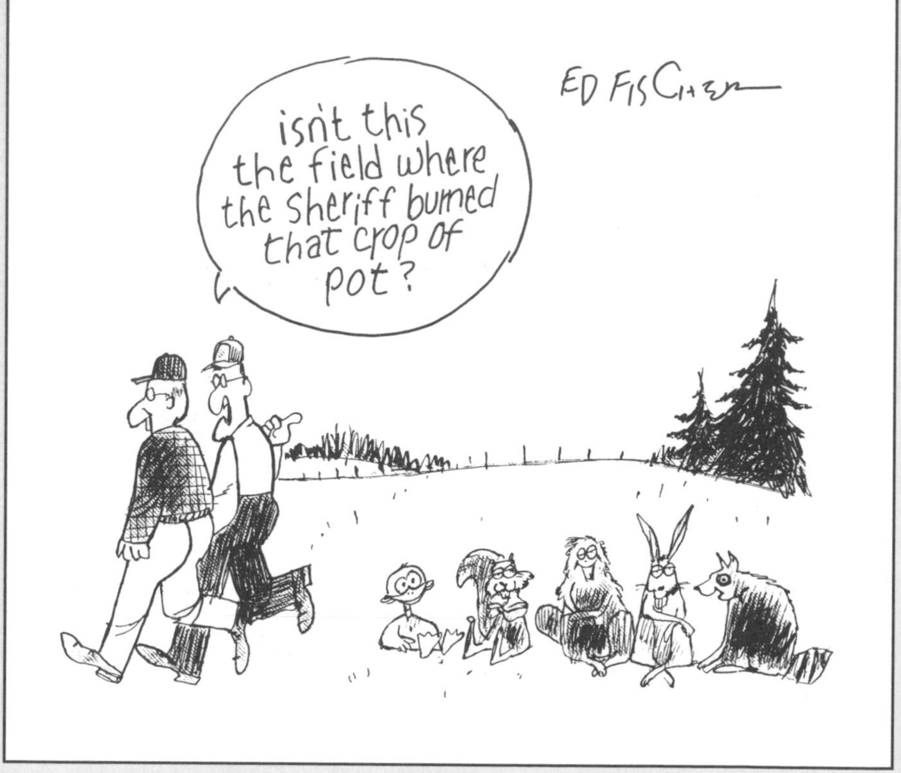
isn't this the field where the sheriff burned that crop of pot?
ED FISCHER

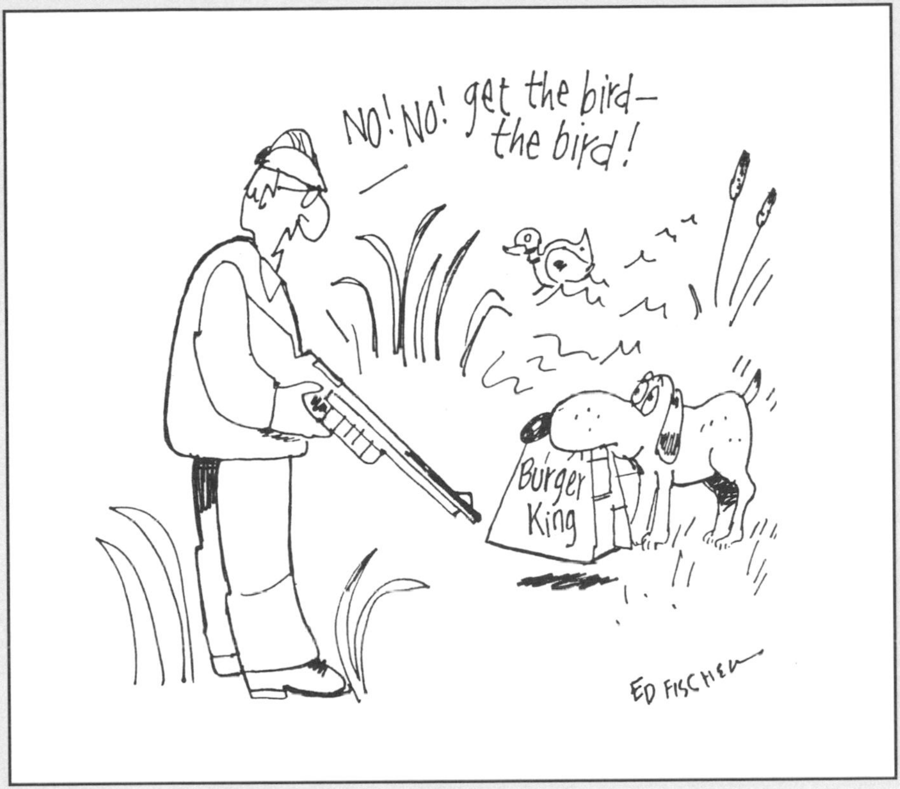
No! No! get the bird—
the bird!
Burger King
ED FISCHER

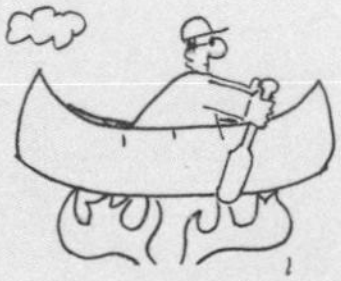

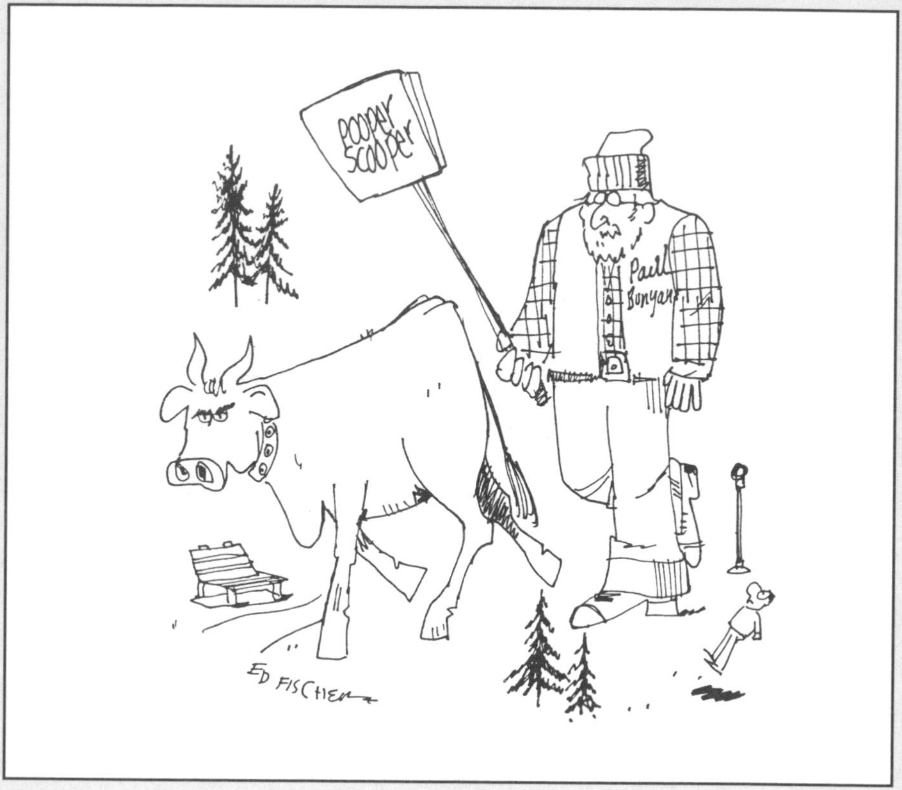

POOPER SCOOPER
Paul Bunyan
ED FISCHER

Dipnet Doug says that fishing is just a matter of timing. You have to get there yesterday.

Two fishing buddies take turns making camp supper. Doug says, "The best things I cook are tuna hot dish and beef stroganoff." Karl replies, "Which is this?"

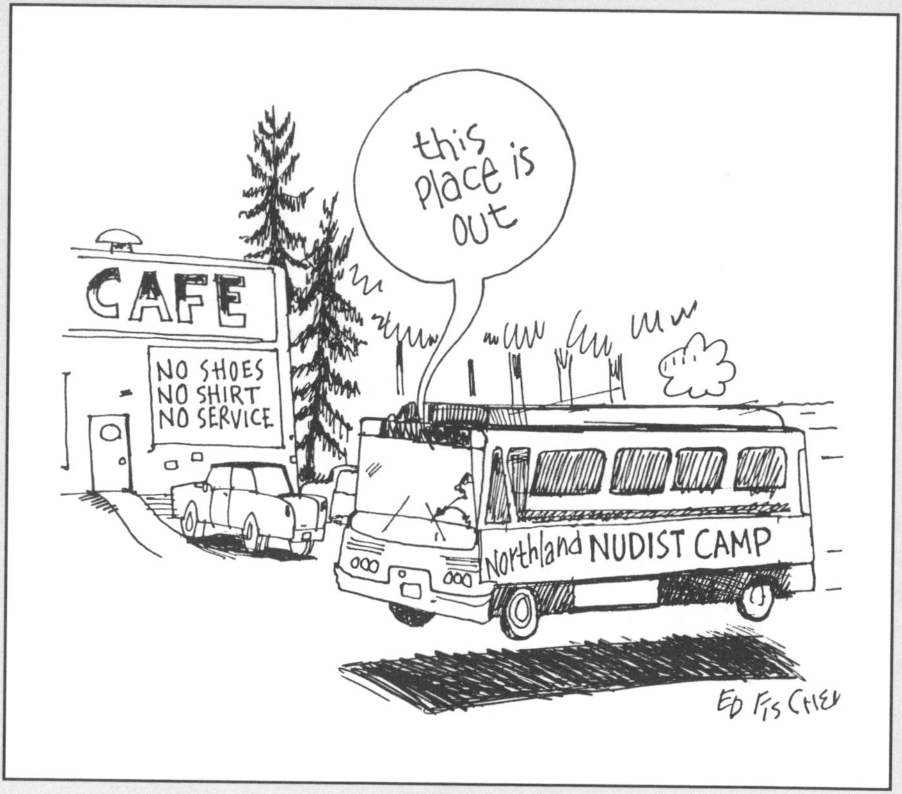
this place is out
CAFE
NO SHOES
NO SHIRT
NO SERVICE
Northland NUDIST CAMP
ED FISCHER

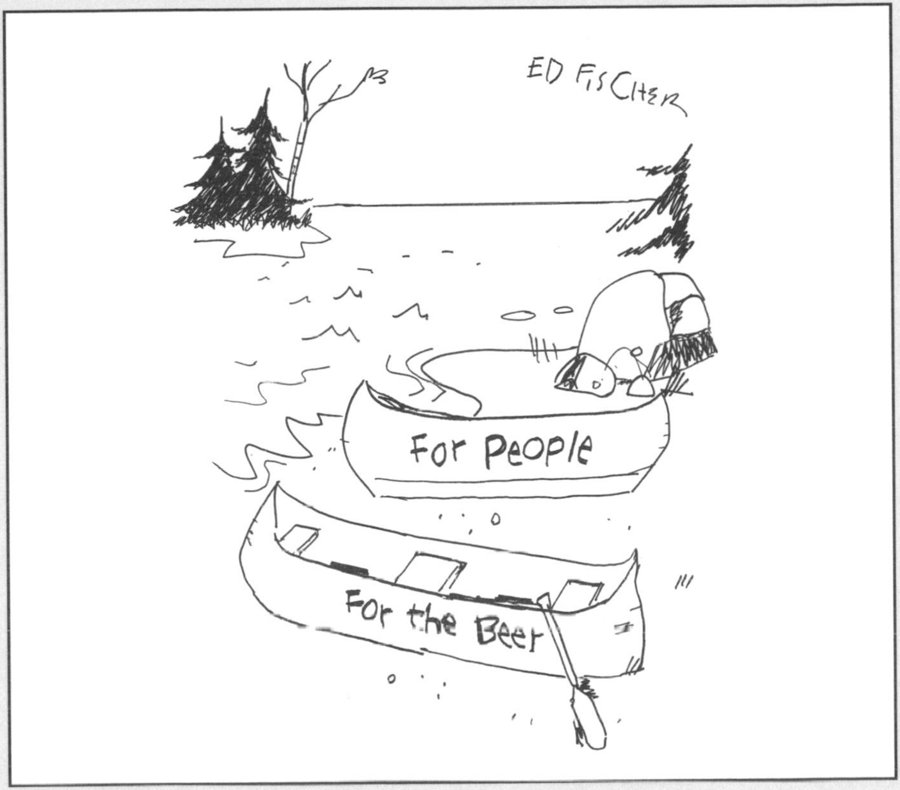
ED FISCHER
For People
For the Beer

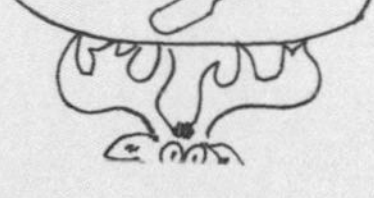

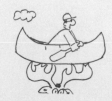

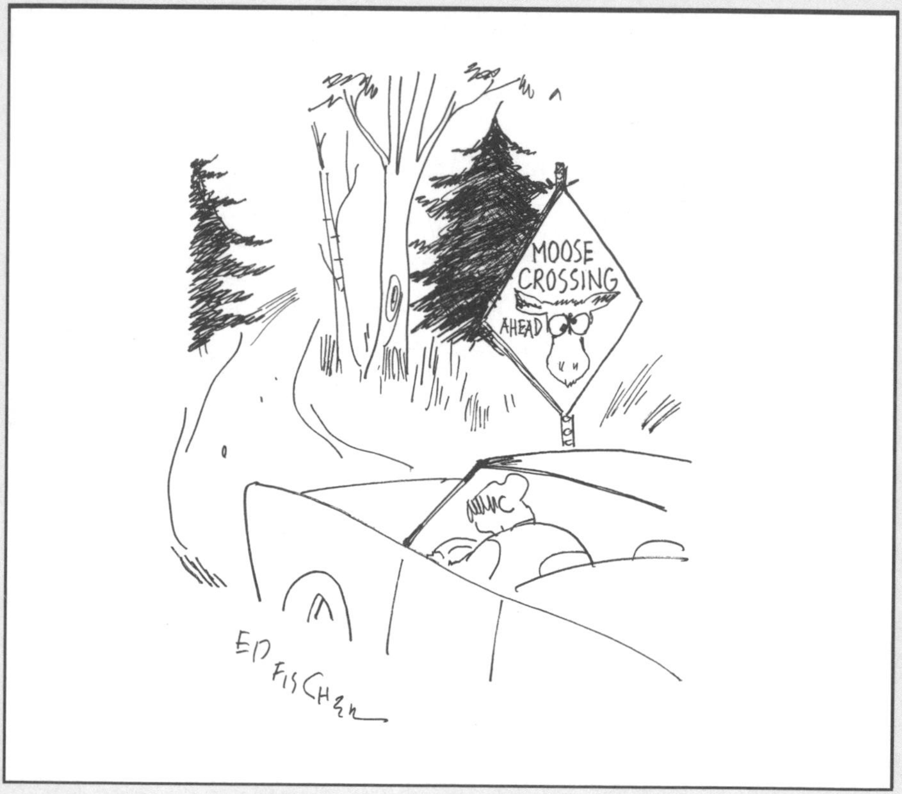
MOOSE
CROSSING
AHEAD
ED FISCHER

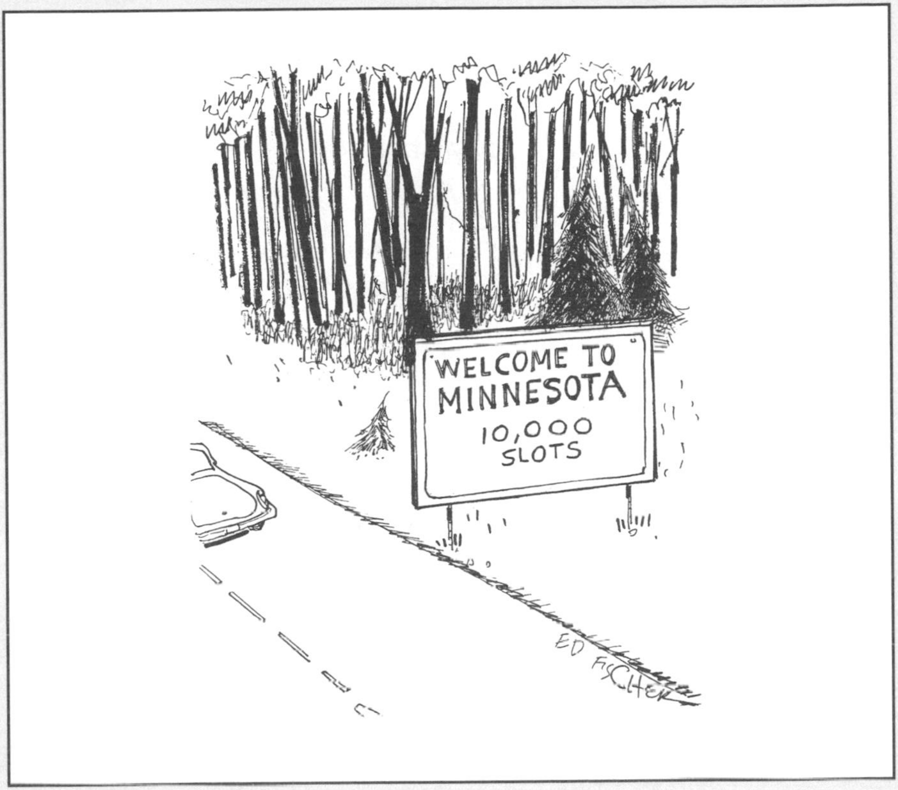
WELCOME TO
MINNESOTA
10,000
SLOTS
ED FISCHER

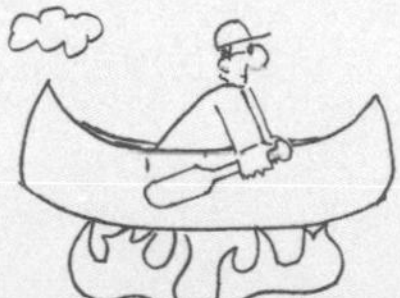

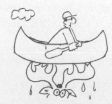

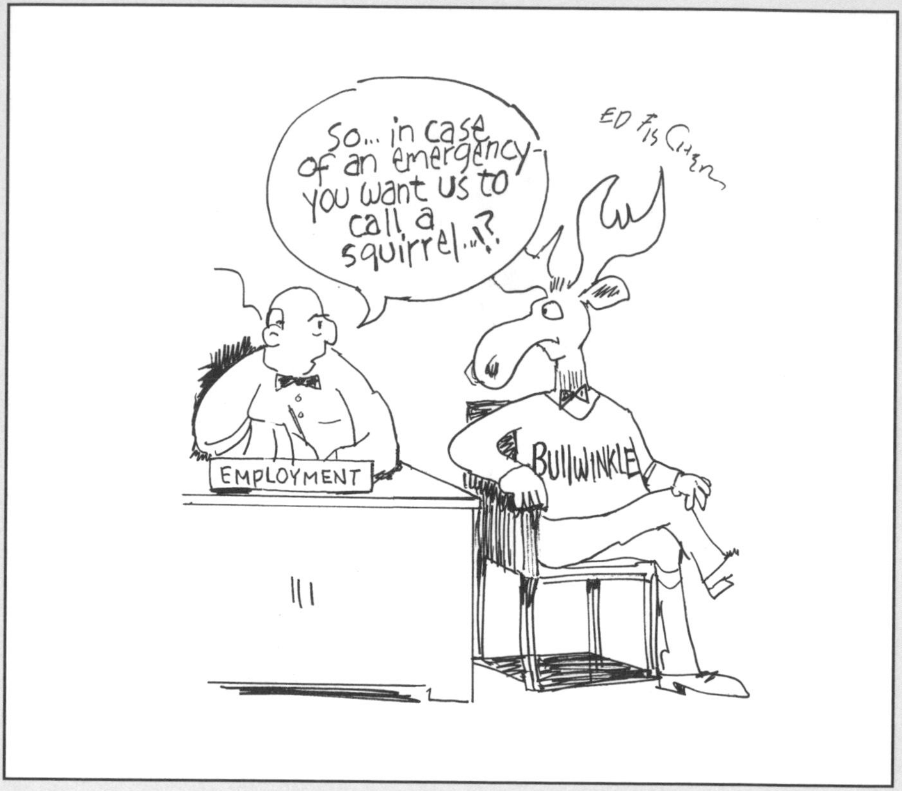
So... in case of an emergency- you want us to call a squirrel..!?
ED FISCHER
EMPLOYMENT
BULLWINKLE

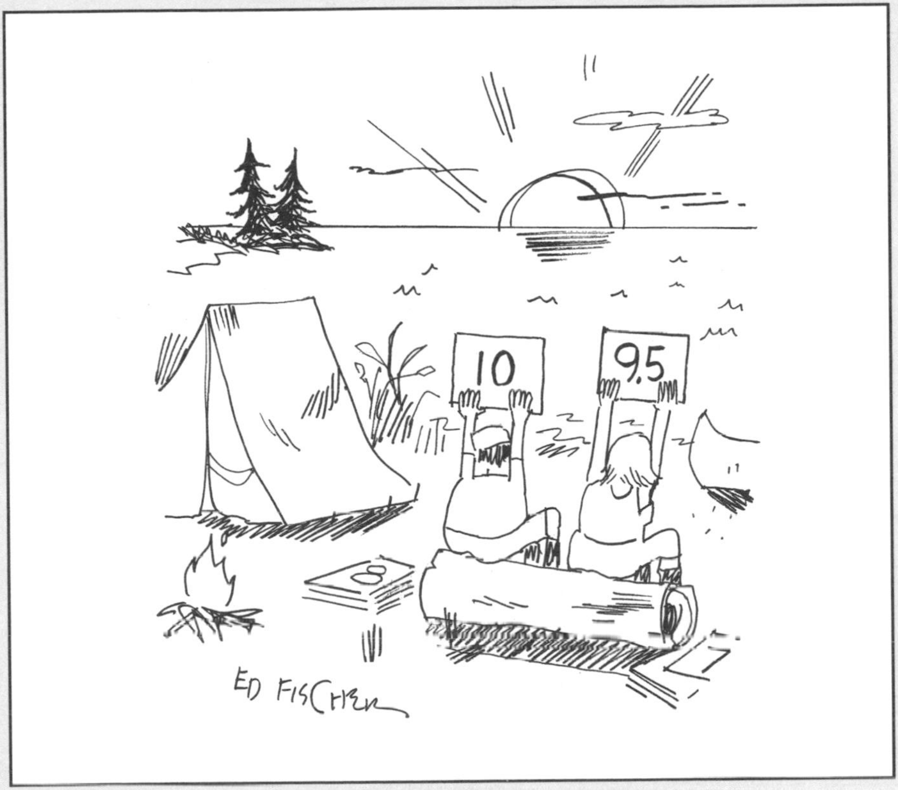
10
9.5
ED FISCHER

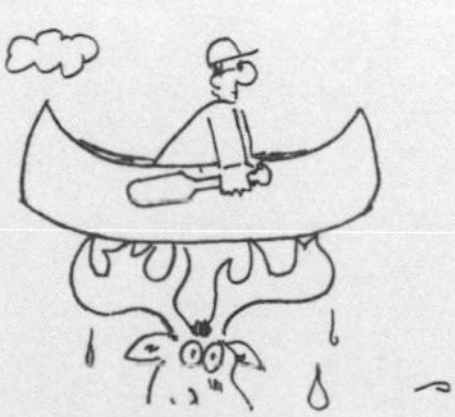

Stranger: "Are the fish biting?" Dipnet Doug: "If they are, they're biting each other."

The mosquitoes are so tough in the Northwoods that, when you slap them, they slap back.

Fishing and camping definition: BEDROCK:
A: Type of stream bottom consisting of rocks. B: Stone or rock under a sleeping bag that keeps you awake.

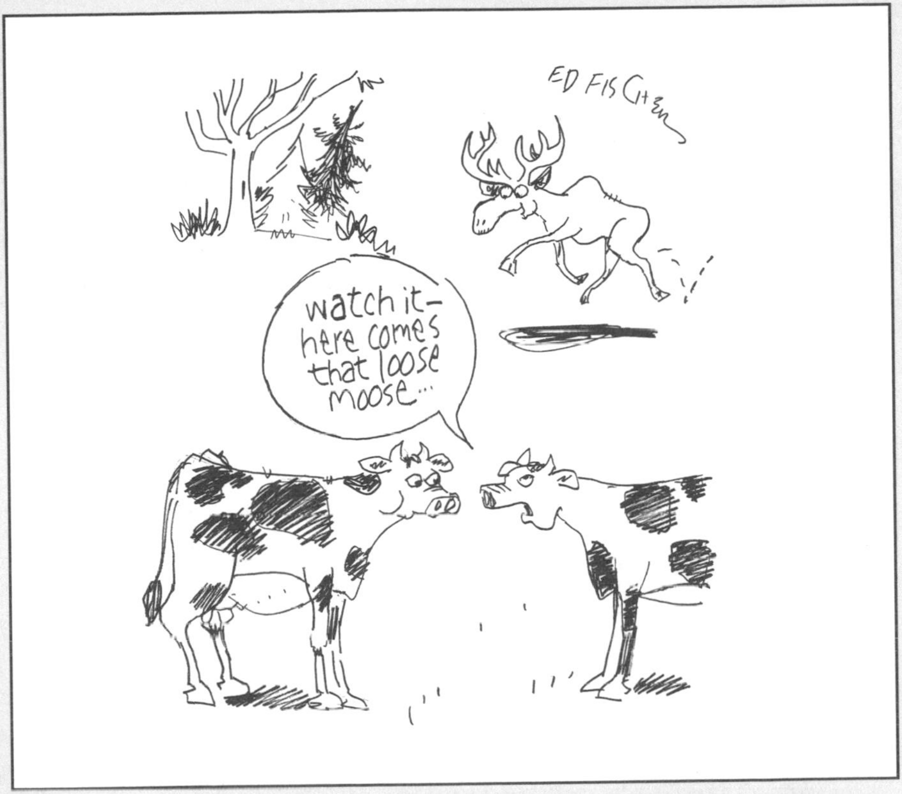
ED FISCHER
watch it-
here comes
that loose
moose...

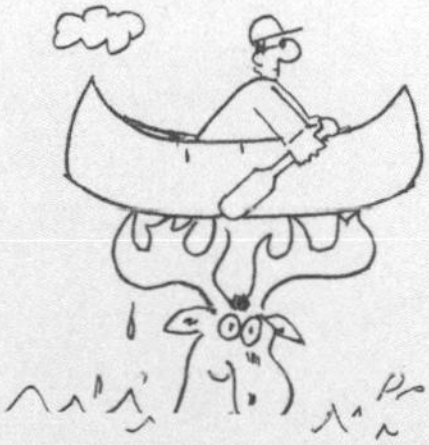

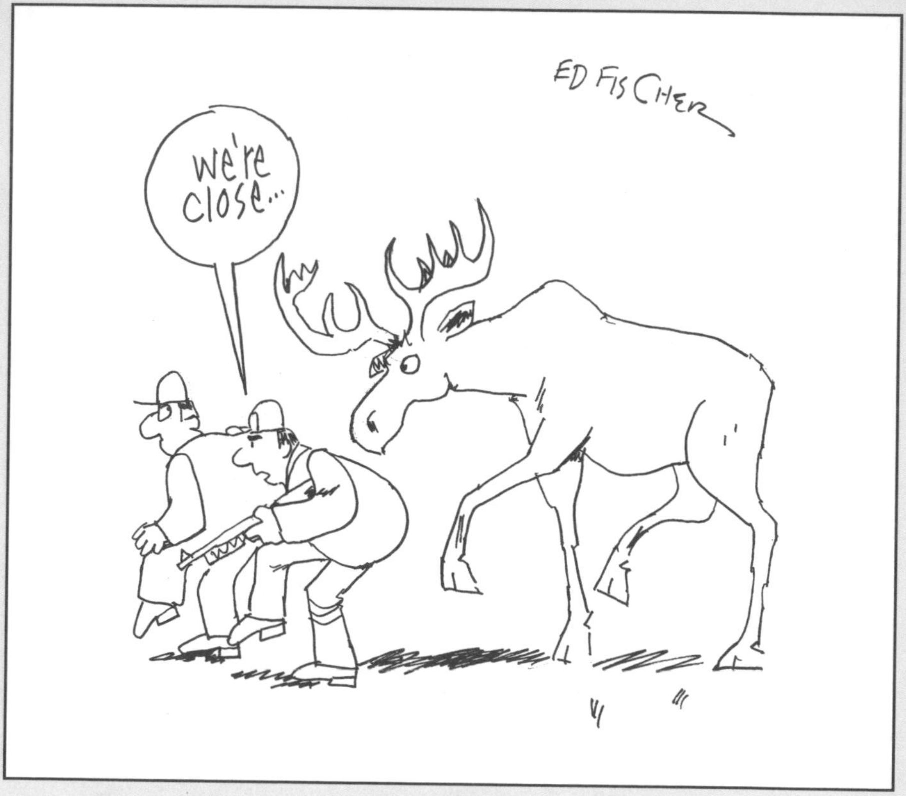
ED FISCHER
we're close...

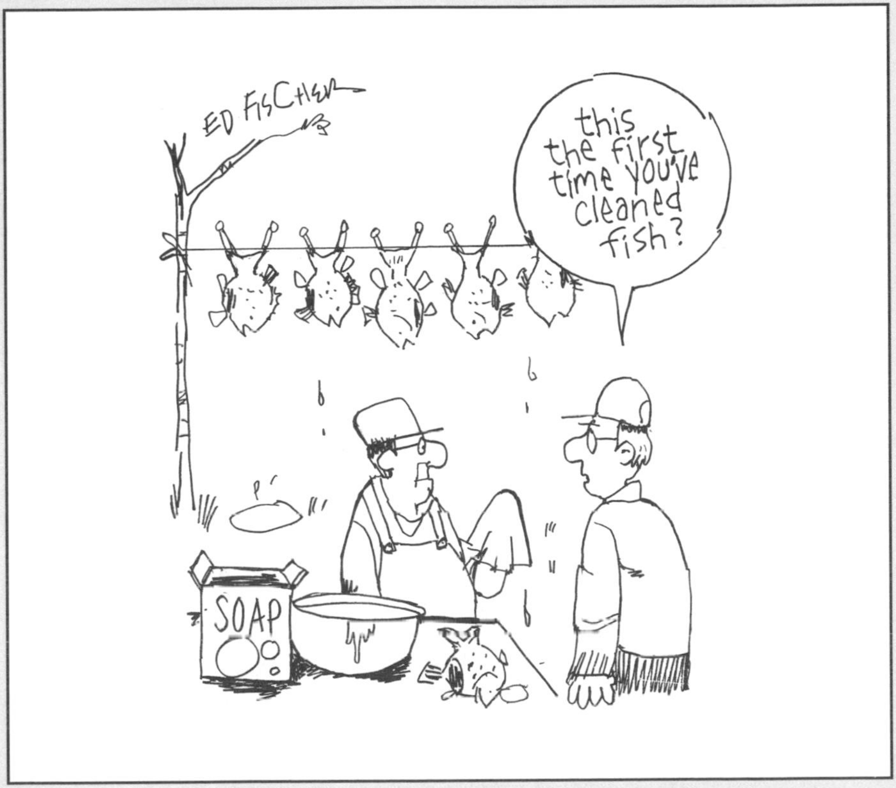
ED FISCHER
this the first time you've cleaned fish?
SOAP

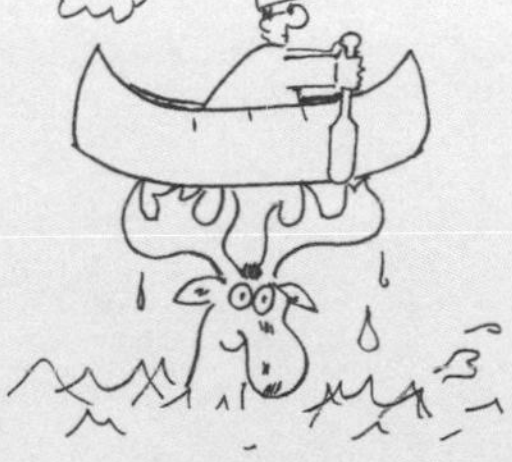

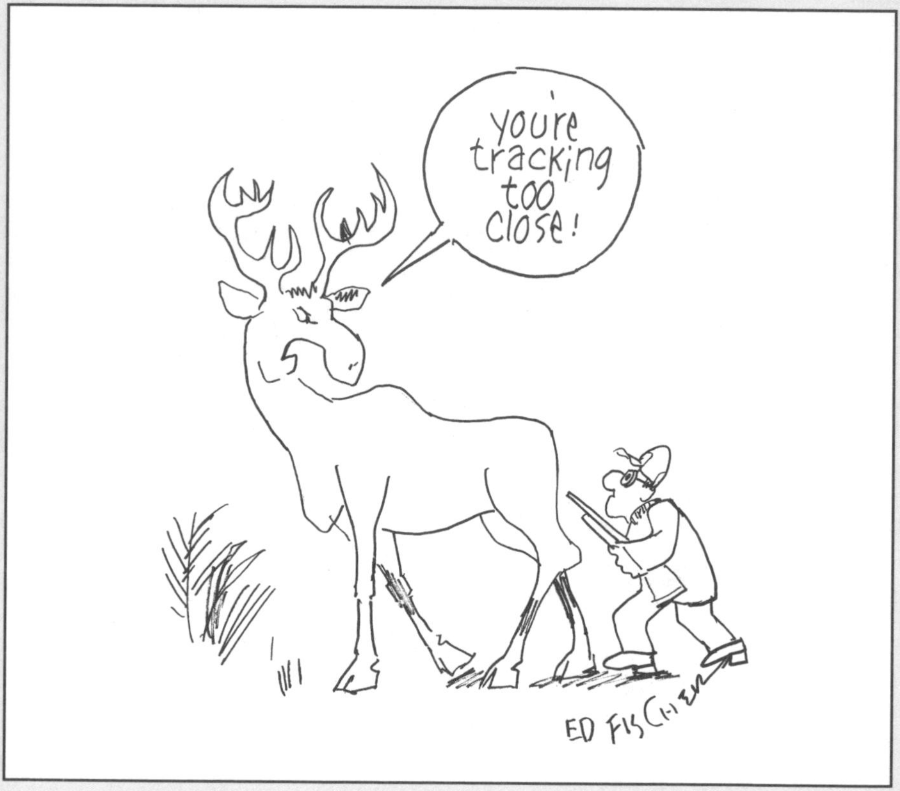
you're tracking too close!
ED FISCHER

The Lakeside Restaurant in Storm Lake charges exorbitant prices. A tourist asked, "What's the catch of the day?" The waiter said, "You are."

Another tourist asked a waitress, "What do you recommend?" She said, "Get out while you still can."

"See this Bearskin rug on the floor?" the old hunter said. "I shot him in northern Wisconsin. It was a case of him or me."

His visitor, bored with his stories, said, "Good thing it was him... not sure you'd make a good looking rug."

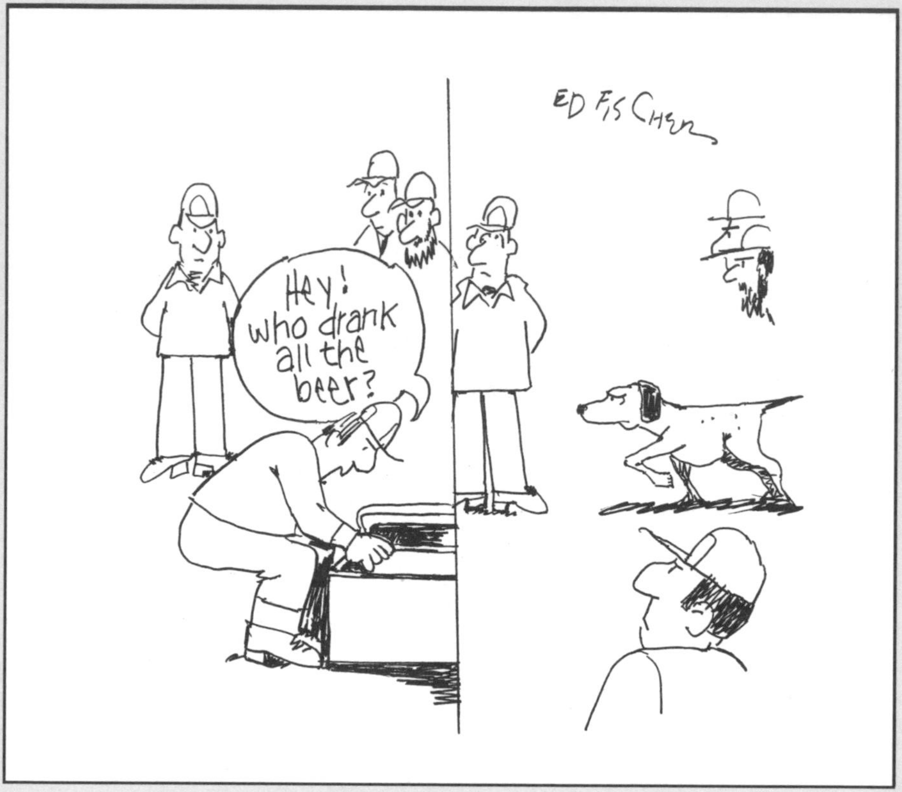
Hey! who drank all the beer?
ED FISCHER

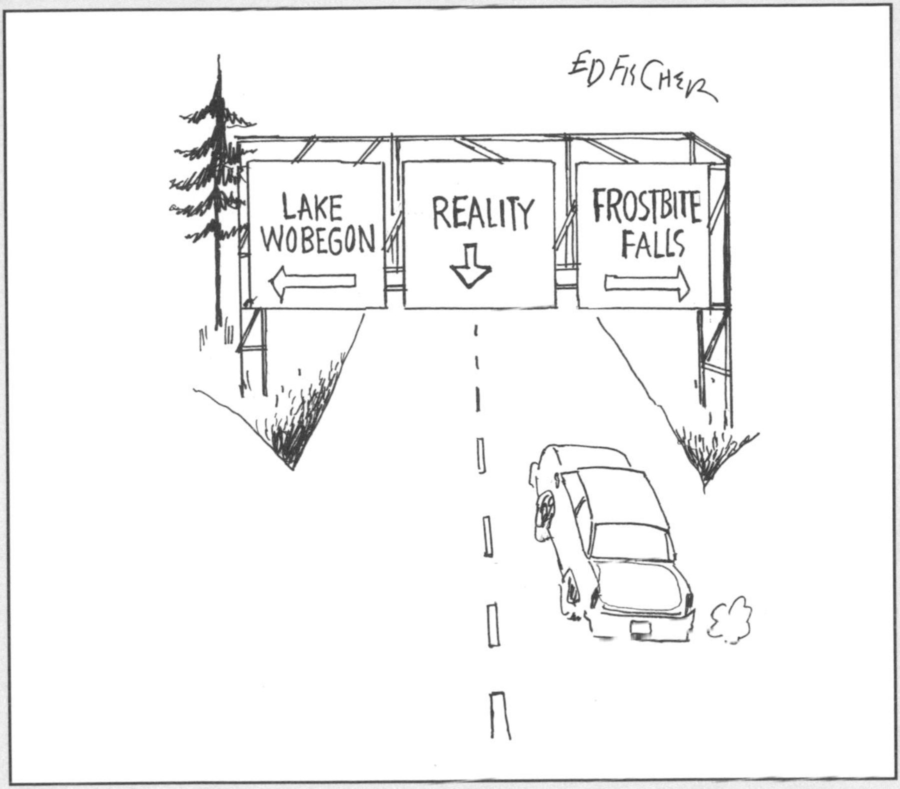
ED FISCHER
LAKE WOBEGON
REALITY
FROSTBITE FALLS

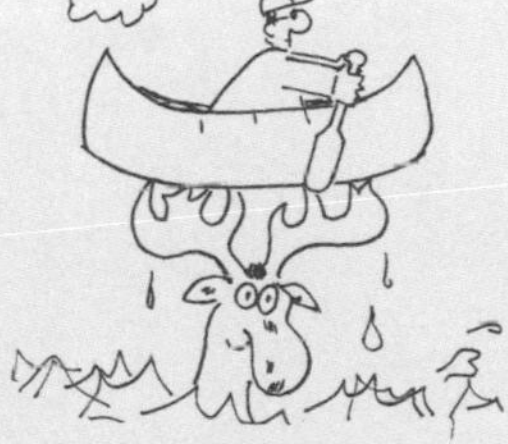

Doreen asked the undertaker, "How much does an obituary cost?"

The undertaker replied, "One dollar per word."

Doreen then said, "I want the obituary to read 'Matt is dead'."

The undertaker was an old fishing buddy of Matt's and was a little disturbed by such a curt obituary, so he offered, "I'll make you a special deal since I knew Matt so well. I'll pay for half of the obituary out of my own pocket."

Doreen's face lit up and she replied, "Great. I want it to read 'Matt is dead. Boat for sale'."

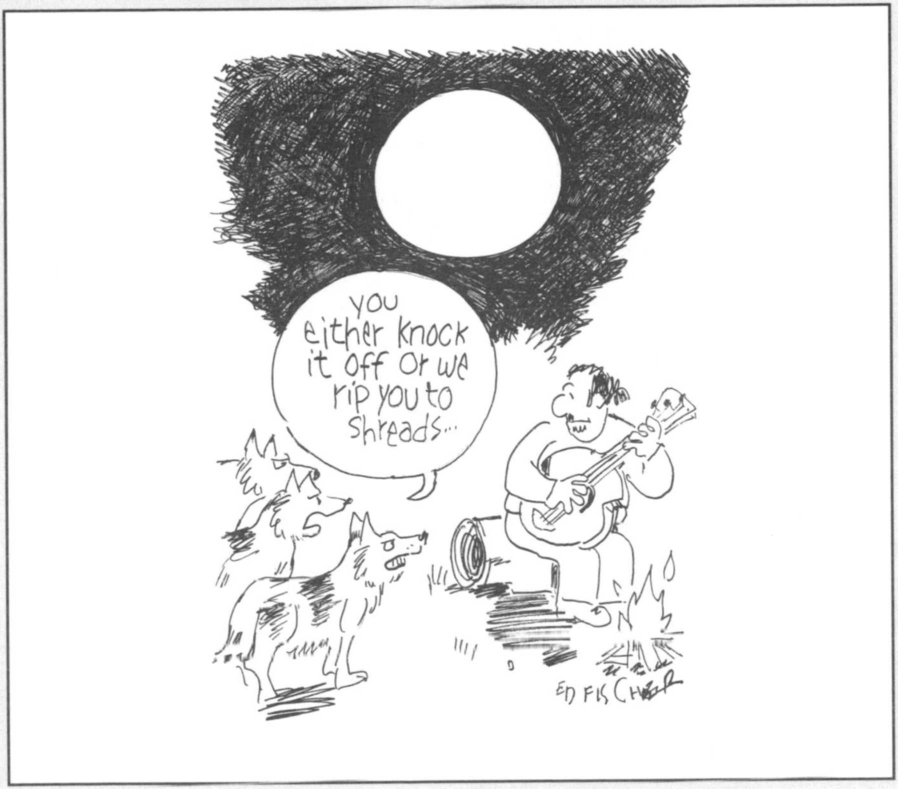
you either knock it off or we rip you to shreads...
ED FISCHER

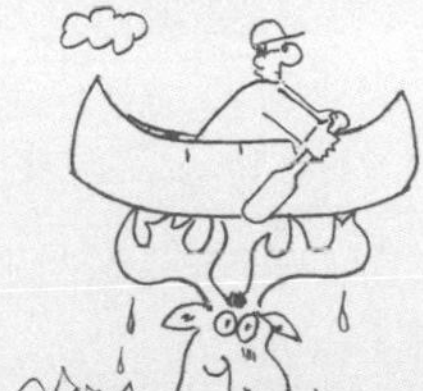

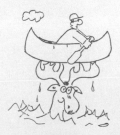

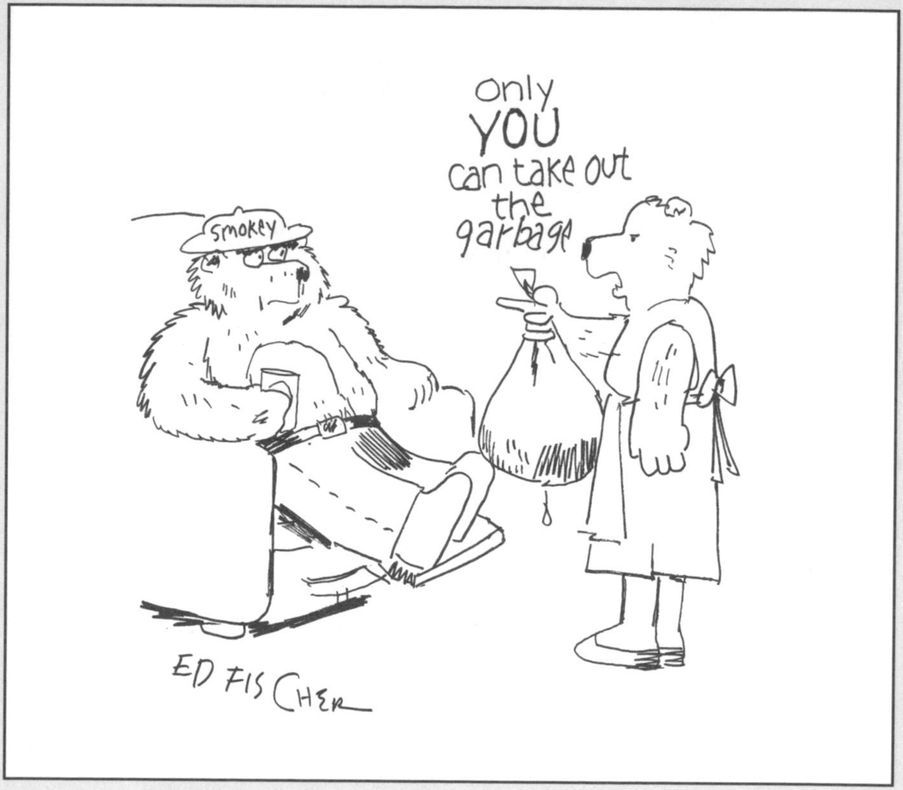

only YOU can take out the garbage
SMOKEY
ED FISCHER

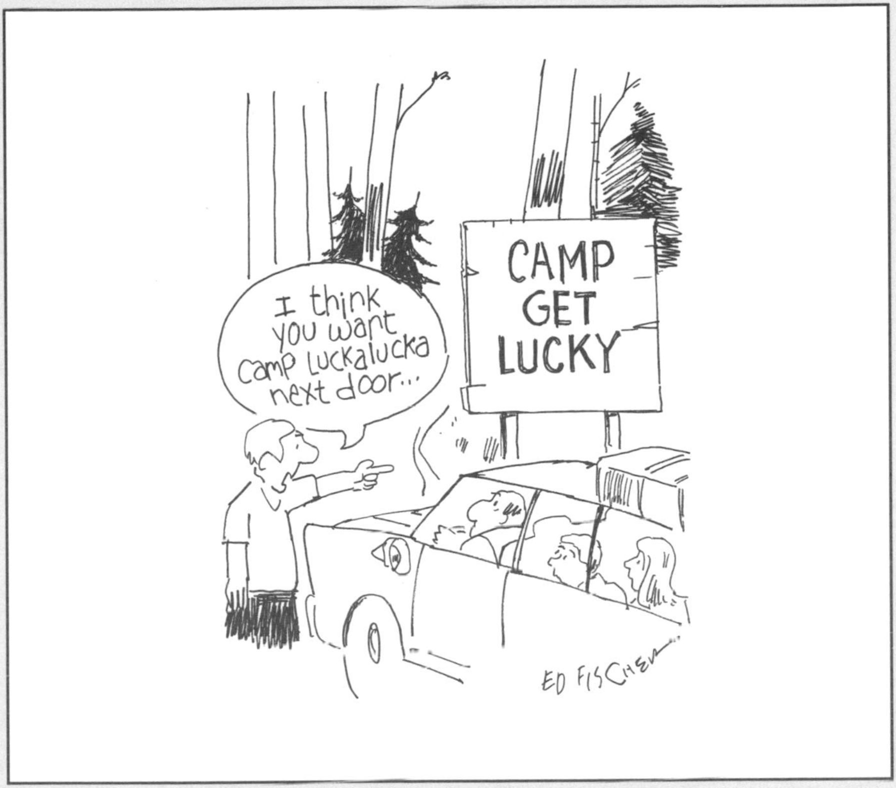
I think you want Camp Luckalucka next door...
CAMP GET LUCKY
ED FISCHER

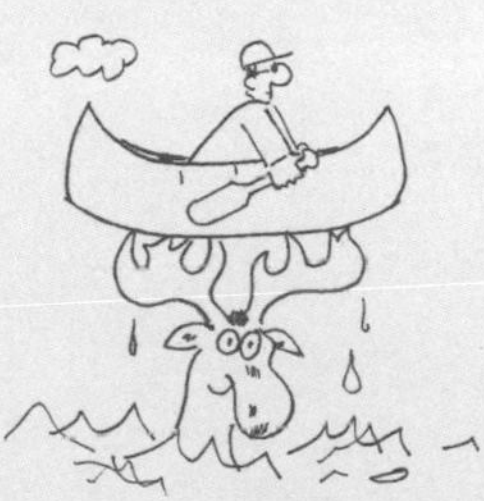

Paul Jr. wrote home from Northwoods Camp: "Please send food. All they serve here is meals."

A camper from New York was bothered by mosquitoes, then a barrage of fireflies. "Great," he said, "now they're coming at me with flashlights!"

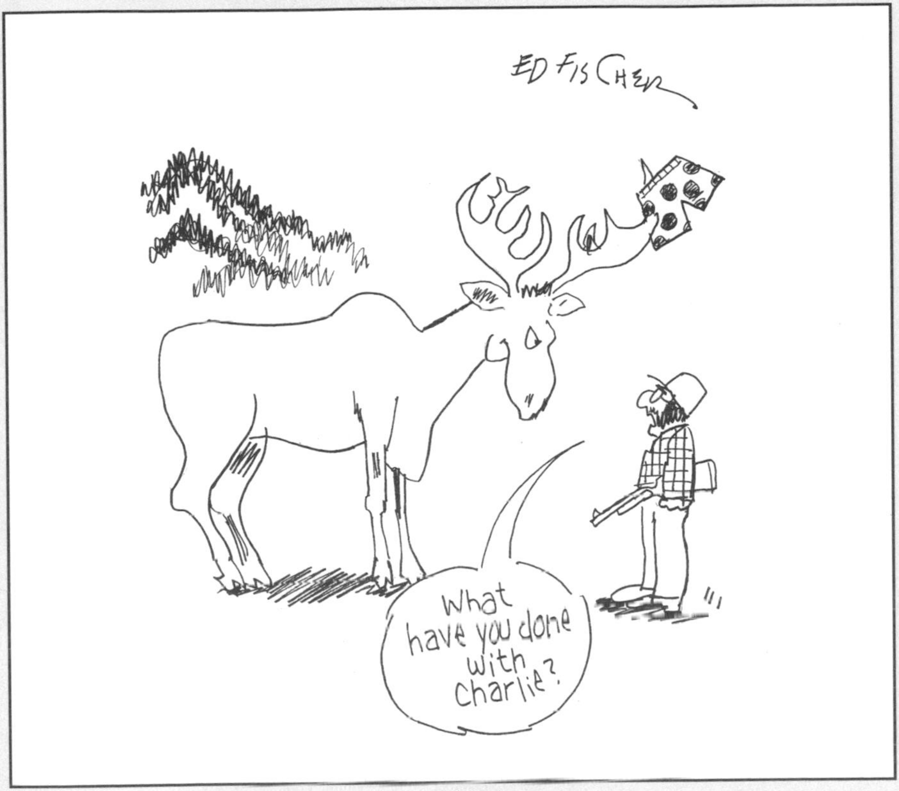
ED FISCHER
What have you done with Charlie?

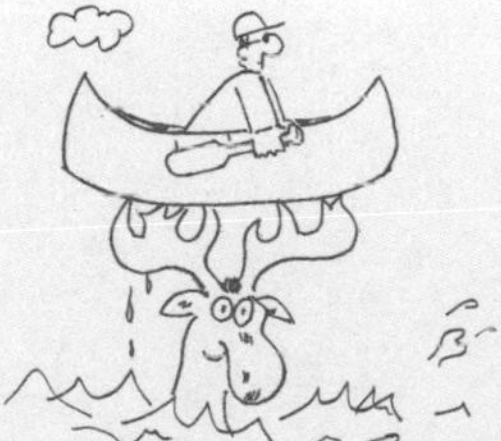

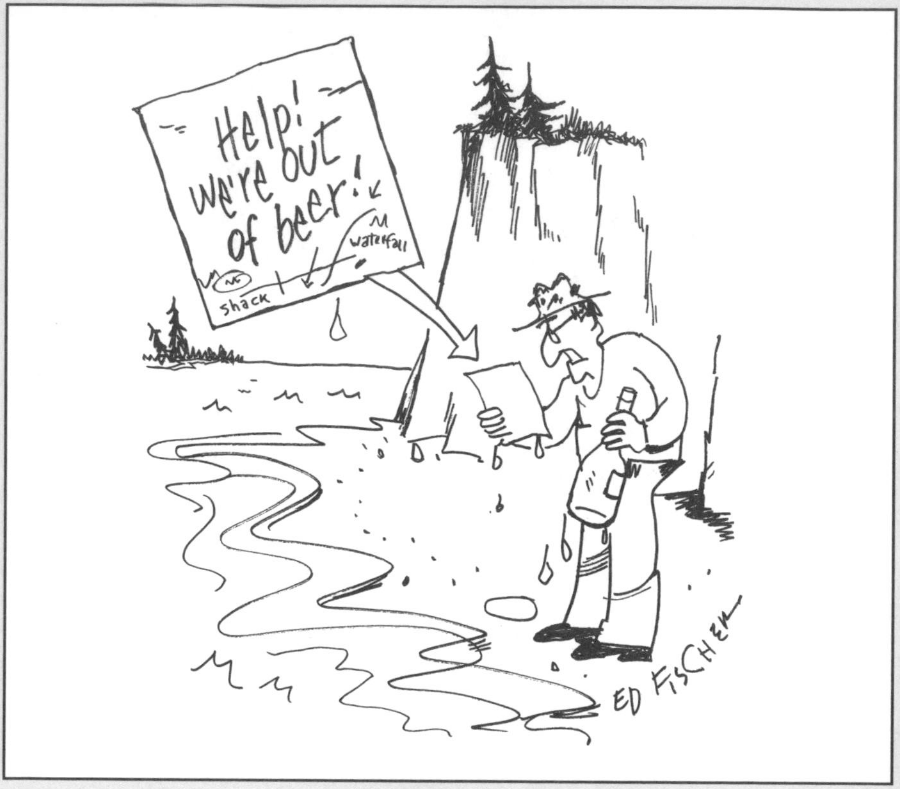
Help! we're out of beer!
waterfall
shack
ED FISCHER